A Grand Tour of Gardens

A Grand

Tour of Gardens

Traveling in Beauty through
Western Europe and the United States

Anne Sinkler Whaley LeClercq

THE UNIVERSITY OF SOUTH CAROLINA PRESS

© 2012 University of South Carolina

Published by the University of South Carolina Press
Columbia, South Carolina 29208

www.sc.edu/uscpress

Manufactured in the United States of America

21 20 19 18 17 16 15 14 13 12
10 9 8 7 6 5 4 3 2 1

Library of Congress Cataloging-in-Publication Data
LeClercq, Anne Sinkler Whaley, 1942–
    A grand tour of gardens : traveling in beauty through Western
Europe and the United States / Anne Sinkler Whaley LeClercq.
        p. cm.
    Includes bibliographical references and index.
    ISBN 978-1-61117-068-9 (cloth : alk. paper)
    1. Gardens—Europe, Western—Anecdotes. 2. Gardens—United
States—Anecdotes. I. Title.
    SB455.L38 2012
    635.094—dc23
                        2011048942

Title spread: *photograph:* A river god at Villa Lante, Bagnaia, Italy;
scroll illustration: © istockphoto.com/Cloudniners

For my family and friends and garden lovers everywhere

Contents

Illustrations

Acknowledgments

My family and friends have inspired me to bring my *Charleston Mercury* articles together as a book. First, I am deeply appreciative to the editor of the *Charleston Mercury,* Charles Waring, who granted permission for the use of my travel essays. My husband, Professor Fred LeClercq, has been an indispensable travel partner. He excels in finding a garden off the beaten track. He enjoys searching for the perfect word to describe each adventure. His passion for history adds perspective and depth to each essay included here. I owe a special note of thanks to Alexander Moore, my acquisition editor of the University of South Carolina Press. He encouraged me to bring these essays together as a coherent whole. In addition, Bill Adams, the managing editor at the press, has been a highly competent and delightful person who has assisted in editing the work.

Prologue

MANY OF THE ESSAYS GATHERED HERE were published originally in the *Charleston Mercury,* a newspaper published twice a month; I have served as newspaper's chief garden and travel correspondent since 2004. My husband, Fred LeClercq, and I have traveled frequently in Europe, with gardens and art as a major focus. These essays provide a roadmap for visiting and enjoying gardens. The focus is the discovery of gardens as a source of art, inspiration, and entertainment; each chapter will touch on garden history, design, and horticulture. My goal is to tempt and inspire the reader to get out into the magic of sun, sky, and garden enjoyment. My hope is to provide us with a garden microscope and a handful of rubrics for assessing the success of each garden in terms of aesthetics and efficacy.

Enjoying a garden requires knowledge of each country's unique national style. It also requires a set of rubrics against which a visitor can gage the effectiveness of a garden's design and horticulture. The tips in these essays will provide a visitor the tools for deciphering the "language" of a garden. No garden is perfect. It is essential in assessing the effectiveness of a design and the robustness of the planting scheme to ask the right questions. Is this an "all at once" formal design that can be comprehended at a single glance? Is this a romantic landscape design with twists and unexpected delights? How has the gardener met adverse conditions of topography, wind, sun, and soil? What devices has the gardener used to meet these challenges? What combinations of plants have been used to develop the horticultural scheme of the garden? Is the final result a garden with pleasing aesthetics in terms of design, color, and plant combinations? What standards are essential to create an architectonic design or floor plan for the garden? Is this a garden that entertains and delights with its sense of immediacy?

The introductory essay, "Gardening as Art and Entertainment," was written by my mother, the late Emily Whaley. Mother shared her wonderful garden at 58 Church Street in Charleston with visitors from all over the world. Her garden gate was always open. She developed a unique palette for creating a garden rich in art and entertainment. She generously shared some of these insights in her book, *Mrs. Whaley and Her Charleston Garden.* Planting her garden with an artist's perception for color and the shapes of plants, she especially loved the combination of blue and pink. In the spring there were blue pansies, blue verbena, pink tulips, and pink camellias. In fall there were blue hydrangeas and pink roses. Mother planted for depth, bringing color up to eye level. She enjoyed the contrast of her smooth and velvety green lawn with the lush flowering of her borders. She delighted in focal points that caught the eye or even surprised; she used her garden pool, and the lovely goose girl that adorned it, as one of those eye-catching spots. It also served to bring flocks of birds into her garden. Mother enjoyed entertaining in her garden. She could be found there in the mornings in her bathrobe, talking to her plants and enjoying a hot cup of coffee. In the afternoon she would sit on her terrace with her Jack Russell terrier, Rosie, talking with friends and visitors and sipping an ice and vodka. Her garden was a place of quiet and repose, away from the planned regime of ordinary life. These beliefs and pointers were shared with her admirers in lectures that the two of us delivered between 1996 until her death in 1998. Emily Whaley's rubrics provide a useful guide for critiquing and admiring gardens. Today the garden is owned by my sister Marty Whaley Cornwell, who uses her artist's touch to change and develop an exciting new palette for the garden at 58 Church St.

As Marty said to me recently: "My hope is that the garden at 58 Church Street will continue to be an inspiration to those who seek solace in the midst of beauty and who wish to create a garden of their own, and that the garden will always be a place where I can be inspired, where my soul can catch up with my body and find sure footing. As plants grow out of scale or die, I want to explore replacing them with ones that will thrive on their own and provide unique qualities—be it leaves, blossoms, scent, or color—that will enhance the entire scope of the garden."

The second introductory essay, "Rules of the Road When Traveling," comes with firsthand experience. Every trip, even the best planned one, can produce an unexpected challenge or a delightful surprise. The immediacy and joy of being in a lovely garden has made traveling to gardens an inspiring focus. I love the feel of wind and sun on my face. I delight in exquisite color schemes that are vibrant and change with the time of day and the season of the year. I search to find the best water garden. I relish the hard work that goes into pruning and maintaining a garden. Most of all I love seeing something totally new. The rush of excitement and the feeling of being alive create an immediate stimulus that plays on for days in my memory. The heart of the book lies in the seven parts incorporating my essays from the *Charleston Mercury*. Each essay will take you on a trip of discovery to a different and new country and to some of the top gardens in the western world. Each provides additional reading and travel tips for enjoying your adventure.

Entrance to Emily Whaley's garden at 58 Church Street, in Charleston, South Carolina.
All photographs are from the author's collection.

An antique garden urn filled with spring blooms from Emily Whaley's garden

Emily Whaley enjoying her colorful perennial border

Reflecting pool and summer blooms in Emily Whaley's garden

Blue hydrangeas and yellow Parkinsonia in Emily Whaley's garden

Spring blooms in Emily Whaley's garden

Garden view from Emily Whaley's terrace

The reflecting pool in Emily Whaley's garden

Part 1

An Overview

VISITING AND ENJOYING GARDENS

Visiting and enjoying gardens is a treasured inheritance that came to me from my mother, Emily Whaley. She summed up her garden lore in her book, *Mrs. Whaley and Her Charleston Garden.* Her insights and rules for creating and perfecting her own garden became mine as I conversed, gardened, and spoke to different groups with her over the years. Later, when I returned to Charleston, the two of us gave many garden talks that were illustrated by images from her garden at 58 Church Street in Charleston, South Carolina.

My mother was funny and loved to tell stories. I have a vivid memory of an experience at a garden talk at the Cloisters at St. Simons, Georgia. At that time we were still using a slide projector that required a darkened room. When we arrived, the room was so filled with windows and light that it would have been impossible to use our illustrated talk. She laughed and said, "Don't worry. I will just tell stories." And that is exactly what she did, pleasing and entertaining our audience.

She shared her passion for gardening with both my sisters Marty Whaley Cornwell and Emily Whaley Whipple. Marty owns and has changed and amplified the garden at 58 Church Street as only another talented painter would do. Emily has a garden at Yeamans Hall in Berkeley County, South Carolina, where mother and Emily created a splendid formal garden surrounded by vistas of woodlands and marsh. Together they amplified views with focal points using antique fountains, urns, and statuary. Mother was also an inspiration to our three sons, Ted, Ben, and Kershaw LeClercq. Each has a garden today, influenced by her garden style. When mother received her first royalties from her book, *Mrs. Whaley and Her Charleston Garden,* she send each son a check to do with as they pleased. Mother was delighted to learn that Ted had used his small check to purchase a load of cow manure for his garden in New Orleans. Ted is still an avid gardener and uses mother's color maxims to create vibrant color combinations including yellow and lavender—and blue and pink—in his borders.

Whenever Fred and I traveled with mother, she carried her paints and paintbrushes and did watercolors of gardens, lakes, and mountains as Fred and I hiked. She loved the mountain and lake vistas glimpsed from balconies. We especially enjoyed staying with mother at the Grand Hotel on Lake Geneva in Switzerland, with its lovely formal gardens and superb restaurant. Another favorite was Leysin, Switzerland, where we journeyed on many occasions. During these trips we conversed about garden styles and history, and I began to appreciate her many insights. Sharing thoughts on gardening, painting, and aesthetics deepened our relationship and enhanced my admiration for her wealth of experience and knowledge. These insights have informed many of my own views about gardening and are reflected in the essays of this book. Mother's essay delves into her suggestions for creating a quality garden. In addition she was a happy traveler and a great companion on any trip. I learned by traveling with her how to appreciate unexpected small delights in new experiences, people, and places. Her breadth of imagination fueled my own love of the untried and unexpected. ∾

Gardening as Art and Entertainment

EMILY WHALEY

Create a garden, and you are instantly immersed in an entertaining and artistic experience. You become enveloped by the sense of sight, sound, touch, and smell. A garden is a delight to the eye, allowing our spirits to soar through deftly controlled spaces. A tuneful garden echoes with the sound of water, birds, frogs, and wind. A tactile garden lures us to touch with its diversity of plants and flowers. An odiferous garden entrances us with the perfume of rose, sweet olive, gardenia, lilac, and mint.

Here are eleven helpful hints to creating the artful and entertaining space of your dreams. These organizational guidelines will help you as you go about the process of choosing plants, tending your landscape, and developing new spaces. Or you might use them as you enjoy your neighbors' gardens. Ask yourself: why is this garden successful? These eleven tips may help you find the answer.

- Plant a boundary planting that encloses your private haven. Use several varieties of plants and trees of various heights and shapes, but predominated by a choice of one evergreen that will give a sense of unity to the whole. The garden at 58 Church Street has a ten-foot-high white fence on one side and camellias on the other, creating a secret garden that enhances the feeling of privacy.
- Create a design with a firm and "at once" noticeable floor plan. Look for good proportions that incorporate your own aesthetic and practical desires. The garden at 58 Church Street fills a thirty by ninety-foot area making a strong statement that combines three types of space: a rectangle, an oval and a circle.
- Use a focal point that is eye catching and clearly established. It can be a statue, bird bath, gazebo, bench, or eye-catching plant. The garden at 58 Church Street has four focal points that lead the eye into the space: an iron gate for welcome; a stone statue at the bend in the walk; a reflecting pond with a goose girl statue at the end of the lawn; and, a deep pond in the sunken garden.
- Develop a stretch of smooth, velvety green grass to give a sense of repose. The froth of multiple colors and plants in the typical perennial border would overwhelm without the soothing center of velvety grass.
- Design paths through your garden as routes of exploration to unexpected venues. The brick walk into the garden at 58 Church Street leads the visitor around the grass and into the sunken garden.

- ❧ Maximize both sun and shade to provide alternatives and variety for planting. The heavily shaded sunken garden at 58 Church Street provides the perfect environment for camellias, azaleas, and hydrangeas.
- ❧ Bring color to eye level. Do not mix color fields: blues, lavenders, purples, and pure pinks or else peach, apricot, and salmon colors. Avoid red. My garden at 58 Church Street shows the magical use of white stocks and white sweet alyssum mixed with blue forget-me-nots, white tulips, and pink verbena. The entrance to the garden at 58 Church Street epitomizes the use of color at eye level with azaleas in pink profusion.
- ❧ Plant for peak bloom in your climate: fall—blue plumbago, Gerbera daisies, roses; winter—camellias, sweet olives; spring—dogwoods, azaleas, tulips, roses, pansies; summer—hydrangeas, Parkinsonia, oleander, vitex, daylily. The garden border at 58 Church Street features peak early spring flowers, and then blooms again in fall.
- ❧ Provide attractive seating for companionship or for just being alone. I have a flagstone patio with comfortable seating for enjoying tea or an afternoon cocktail. Rosie and I sit in the garden alone watching for lizards, bees, or frogs.
- ❧ Remember that water, moving or still, creates small adventures from birds, frogs, and children. The gurgle of water from my lover's lane fox lights up the space with the sound of splashing water.
- ❧ Pay attention to constant and judicious pruning. Get rid of tired, old plants. Simply dig them up and replace them. Bring in the limb cutters to keep your heavens open. Prune with a vengeance to enhance new growth and create a mass of dense blooms. Fertilize heavily every fall.

Rules of the Road When Traveling and a Visit to Dunrobin Garden

INDEED IT IS A CHALLENGE FOR AN AMERICAN to stay on the left-hand side of the road in Scotland, England, Wales, and Ireland. The deeper question is how does one arrange a harmonious trip? We are all so used to our daily work and home patterns that a trip can pose significant challenges that might ruin the anticipated adventure.

I remember traveling with my father, Ben Scott Whaley, to Paris in 1974. It was a trip organized by Sweet Briar College and there were many of my old and young friends aboard. I sat next to my godmother, Louisa Rivers Hagood on the flight over, and I recall her agony when our crew gave all orders in Spanish. She said, "My word, Angie, what will we do if we crash into the sea? We will surely be lost!" On arrival I found my father, Ben Scott Whaley, looking equally agonized. He demanded, "Daughter, find me the best bottle of gin available, and do it quickly!" And when my sister Emily organized an art-filled trip to the Louvre, Ben Scott took one look at all the paintings by Degas, Monet, and Renoir and stated, "This is not for me, I will sit right here until you two return." However, that evening he had organized a trip to the Folie Bergere. His eyes sparkled with delight at the cancan, and he cheered when a water-filled tank was rolled on stage and within was a lovely girl and dolphin. The dolphin successfully removed the enchantress's top piece to the mermaid's bathing suit! The first rule for the road might be "Follow your own dream" or "To each his own." Such a rule could produce a rather solo experience, and surely there is better than that on a well-organized adventure.

That same trip to Paris produced a delightful luncheon with Juliet Staats, the wife of Phil Staats, neighbors of my parents on Church Street, at a charming restaurant in the Marais. Everyone gathered, and we told stories of Charleston, shared accounts of beautiful museums visited, and the delight of the new and different. The setting was convivial, and there was enormous fun in the sharing of stories. The second rule for the road might be "Delight in good food and companionship."

The unexpected is always near when one is in a foreign land; there are many pitfalls to avoid. I remember well traveling with Sweet Briar to Sicily. The last morning at breakfast I bit into a piece of glass. The resulting flow of blood from my tongue was astonishing. Dr. William Wilson, also on the trip with his lovely wife, Margaret, applied iced compresses to no effect, all the while assuring me, "Angie you are not going to die." We ended up in a Sicilian hospital, which looked like a morgue. A bandage of gauze was applied to my tongue, and in about five minutes all the bleeding stopped. I looked at my mate and said, "Let's get out of here." The third rule of the road might be "Expect the unexpected."

There is the delight in a change of scenery and the extravagant bounty of a trip. On a trip to Providence and Newport, a luncheon was planned at the wonderful New York City Yacht Club. We stood on the bluff overlooking the magnificent Newport harbor, filled with sailing ships. We laughed in the sun, and we enjoyed the companionship of so many friends. A fourth rule for the road might be "Relish the change of pace, the new, and the different."

Everywhere we travel we see grandparents and parents traveling with their off-spring. There is an obvious sharing of the lore of generations and a learning environment that is filled with youthful enthusiasm. Once, several years back, we joined our son Kershaw LeClercq and his friend James Ravenel on their trip around South America. Puerto Monte in Chile is in the middle of exquisite volcano territory. As we traveled up over the Continental Divide to Argentina, the young men shared stories of adventures on surfboards and on shipboard around the Cape of Good Hope. Their delight in the people and their culture was infectious. In the wilds on a back road, we soon had a flat tire. We were rescued by a local mechanic whose shop was filled with tempting centerfolds from *Playboy* magazine. We paid him off with a six pack of beer! The fifth rule for the road might be "Travel with your youth."

A sixth and final rule for the road is "Have a learning goal for each trip." I always yearn to discover an enchanting new garden filled with the sound of water. Our destination in July of 2008 was Inverness. The public library there is a fine center for genealogical research. After homework was completed, we visited Dunrobin, the 1848 castle of the Sutherlands on the North Sea. The magnificent, French-style garden was created by Robert Lorimer. The garden is an unexpected surprise as it lies to the east, behind the castle and down a steep cliff. The garden was a sandy seaside eons ago. Over the ages it has been built up with earth. The gardener Iain Crisp, who had cared for these marvelous spaces for ten years, told me that the tow-ering blue lupines, orange lilies, and pink peonies were the result of chicken manure and the warming influence of the Gulf Stream. We had the unique plea-sure of an hourlong hawk and falcon demonstration by Andy Hughes. His wonder-fully trained peregrine falcon flew among us and caught bits of chicken in mid-air. This amazing garden is only two degrees lower than Greenland and on the same latitude as Leningrad. Visiting the Dunrobin garden was a learning experience; not only did I meet the chief gardener, whose wealth of knowledge still inspires me, but I also stored away pictures of the design and planting scheme that will always inform my vision of the perfect garden. The garden is best viewed from the castle. The east-walled garden has three parterres, each surrounding a pool and fountain. This decorative and colorful garden is a fitting foreground to the panoramic view across the Moray Firth to the distant Cairngorm Mountains. Making my way down into the garden, I found a jewel full of flowers, color, and birdsong.

As you travel, visiting and exploring gardens worldwide, you will create your own sense of what fits, what feels right. Many find an organized adventure to their liking, and so book a cruise or a tour. Others find a rental for a week and enjoy getting to know and feel another culture. Because moving on is so often fraught with new challenges, I try to stay in one delightful hotel, preferably surrounded by a garden, for at least two, maybe three, nights. Traveling can inspire new skills and talents. You may polish your photography skills. You may relearn French, German, Spanish, or Italian. You may sink into a great novel. Whatever you do or learn, travel can make you young and dust off the explorer in your genes.

Part 2

Italian Gardens

FROM RENAISSANCE INSPIRATION
TO ROMANTIC INTUITION

Italian gardens find inspiration from the classical model of Rome as revitalized by the Renaissance. In the following ten essays we visit every part of the Italian peninsula, from Sicily in the south to Lakes Como and Maggiore in the north. Italian gardens epitomize a mood of clarity and potency. Much of that mood is created by a single-point perspective design and the use of ornamentation. Ornaments in Italian gardens come in all types and sizes, including fountains, water stairways, balustrades, garden houses, statues, vases, and pergolas. Ornaments are used in Italian gardens as focal points to catch the eye and as devices for creating a mood. They provide unity and clarity to a composition and a solid, inorganic presence in an ever-changing landscape. In every Italian garden, ask these two questions: How are ornaments being used to create a stage set? Does this composition work? The garden at Villa Lante at Bagnaia shows off the Italian vocabulary of ornament and design. The Pegasus statue and fountain by Giambologna at the entrance is dominating and powerful. It sets a mood of magic and potency for its garden.

The other constant element in any Italian garden is the challenge of topography and climate. Italy abounds in hillsides and mountains. Italian garden designers have employed natural settings to great efficacy. Again, Villa Lante is a prime example of a single-point perspective design laid out on a hillside axis. From the ornamental pool at the bottom of the hillside, enriched with sculptures of the four Moors, the garden stairs ascend to a lovely cascade with statues of the River Gods protecting the waters. From the River God fountain, the stairs ascend to the Fountain of the Dolphins, a symbol of faith for Christians. The effect of this garden is one of great control and rationality. This garden is changeless through the seasons, except for light and shadows, and is featured in the essay on Italian Renaissance Gardens. We will also visit some of Italy's top gardens including Sacro Bosco, Villa d'Este, Villa Adriana, Villa Aldobrandini, La Pietra, and Isola Bella.

In addition there are visits to the great gardens of Tuscany in Siena, Fiesole, Florence, and Lucca. The countryside of Tuscany with its vineyards, olive orchards, cornfields, and poppy-covered slopes is enchanting. These gardens and villas are in sympathy with their countryside and provide a bridge between villas and surrounding nature. The rich valley of the Arno becomes a focal point for many of the gardens of Fiesole. These gardens use evergreens, stone, and water to create a garden plan. Frequently there is a series of garden rooms connected by vistas. Our visits include such elegant Tuscan gardens as Villa Gamberaia, Villa I Tatti, Le Balze, Villa Medici, Villa San Michele, and Villa La Pietra, all in the countryside near Florence. Also included are Villa La Foce and Villa Chigi Cetinale near Siena. Close to Lucca are Villa Camigliano and Villa Massei, as well as this charming walled city itself.

The lakes of northern Italy are clear, reflecting a vibrant sky. The gardens dotting the shoreline take full advantage of the lakes masquerading as a mirror. The reflections of clouds, of mountains, and of birds fill the atmosphere. These are garden lovers' lakes with snowy mountains, a reminder of glaciers. From Bellagio a ferry provides access to Villa Monastero, Villa d'Este, Villa Melzi, Villa Balbianello, and Villa Carlotta, each with a magnificent and unique garden. These gardens show the Italian talent for cultivating early spring plantings of rhododendron and azaleas.

Finally, the path leads to gardens on Italy's wonderful islands of Sicily, Capri, and Ischia. "Gardening and Dining by the Sea" captures the essence of the challenges posed, as well as the delights of Italy's many seaside gardens. William and Susana Walton's garden, La Mortella on Ischia, is a perfectly planted garden with more than eight hundred species of rare plants surrounded by fountains, water lilies, hummingbirds, date palms, and olive trees. The garden takes full advantage of the volcanic rocks that dot its hillsides. ❧

Finding Inspiration and Art
in the Gardens of Palermo, Sicily

MARCH COMES IN LIKE A LION, and in Sicily torrents of rain, high winds, and snow proved the proverbial nostrum to be true. Fred and I arrived in Rome, rented a car, and headed to Naples to take the ferryboat overnight from Naples to Palermo, Sicily. That evening we boarded a huge ferry loaded with tractor-trailer rigs and found our snug cabin. The full moon of February lit our way across the Tyrrhenian Sea, and morning found us in the "calla," or old harbor, of Palermo. We found our hotel, the Mondello Palace in a quiet old seaside town of the same name, Mondello, some four miles out of the bustle of Palermo.

We had come to Sicily anticipating seeing the remains of once-thriving Greek settlements dating from the sixth century B.C. Our first visit was to Selinunte on the Mediterranean Sea on the southwest coast of Sicily. We observed fallen columns, solitary foundations, dismantled towers, and wall remnants, with an incredible Doric temple still standing. All around were the remains of a proud and prosperous Greek community founded around 570 B.C. More than two hundred thousand inhabitants lived here until the city was razed in a siege by the Carthaginians in 409 B.C. The yellow limestone columns took on a peachy glow as the sun appeared by magic, turning the sea a green-blue aqua.

Another day we ventured out to Segesta, a jewel of a Greek town that thrived in northwest Sicily in the fourth century B.C. We drove across rolling lands green with wheat, vineyards, and olive orchards. Standing alone against a vast grand canyon was an exquisite Doric temple which towered over the countryside. Black ravens flew and cawed among the ruins. Thucydides reported that after the Trojan War the exiled Phrygians came to Sicily and founded Segesta. It was even thought that the Trojan hero Aeneas arrived in Segesta. As evening fell, we sat in the Greek theater, which snuggled back into the mountainside and looked outward to a vast expanse of snowcapped mountains with the Tyrrhenian Sea in the distance.

Sicily has seen many rulers. The Greeks were successively replaced by the Romans, who were followed by the Byzantines, the Muslims, and the Norman French.

We visited three ancient Norman churches, each a Romanesque jewel. The interiors glowed with golden mosaics telling the stories of the Bible. The apse of the Palatine Chapel, built in 1129, was dominated by a figure of Christ with outstretched arms. His red and gold tunic was the color of the ethereal God, while his blue mantle signified the cloak of man. This dramatic and dominating image of Christ was visible again in the Cathedral of Monreale built in 1174, high on a hill over Palermo, and in the Norman Church of Cefalù built in 1131. The fourteen-carat gold mosaics fill each of these churches with an iridescent shimmering light.

The Norman French conquerd Sicily in 1063, thereby ending more than two hundred years of Islamic rule. Cefalù had been under Byzantine domination prior to its conquest by Muslims in 858. The Byzantine culture in Sicily was not extinguished by two centuries of Islamic and then Norman French governance. Therefore Cefalù Cathedral, begun in about 1131 by Roger II, brother of William the Conqueror, although Norman or Romanesque in architectural style, contains mosaics from about 1148 that are fine examples of early Byzantine art, especially the large Panocrator mosaic in the apse of royal blue on a field of real gold.

We journeyed to the interior town of Corleone, made famous by the Godfather films. The town sits on a fertile farming plateau, once isolated in the interior of Sicily. An impressive highway with tunnels and arched bridges now brings this farming center closer to civilized Sicilian life. The classic red wine of this region, Nero d'Avola, is characterized by its intense ruby color and a flavor of aromatic herbs. The dry and fruity white wines were served at the winery where we stopped for lunch. We were served delicious antipasti including eggplant, mushrooms, and sweet red peppers, followed by tomato glazed crostini, fried cheese, and a frittata of vegetables and onions, followed by grilled sausages and potatoes swimming in butter.

Palermo is majestic in its eighteenth- and nineteenth-century "old town" that fronts a superb natural harbor. Headlands rising to rocky promontories protect each flank, Mt. Pellegrino to the west, and the Conca d'Oro (the shell of gold, so called because of the orange and yellow fruit orchards) to the south and east. The sea is alternately gray, black, sky blue, and light green. We visited the famous Baroque churches, San Giuseppe and Santa Caterina and La Martorana. At the center of these churches was the Fountain of Shame, so called because the beautiful women on the fountain were all naked and covering their beauty spot with their hands.

We visited three diverse gardens in Palermo: the English Garden, the Villa Giulia, and the Botanical Garden. The English Garden with its artificial hillocks, circular fountain, and clumps of trees was designed in 1825 by an architect, Giovani Battista Filippo Basile. It was intended to resemble a romantic English garden but has a formal aspect with statues of Sicilian greats such as the writer Pirandello. There are gigantic date palms and smaller palms of every variety. The garden for the Villa Giulia dates from 1777. It has a neoclassical gate on the seafront with Doric columns, eagles, and coats of arms. Goethe spent part of his afternoons walking along the geometrical paths lined with marble statues. The huge fruited date palms with orange branches and purple fruit provide a counterpoint to the very formal garden. The Botanical Garden, laid out in 1795, covers five acres and has more than twelve thousand different plants from all over the world. There is an enormous variety of grapefruits, oranges, and lemons, including the ruby red Sicilian orange that has a sweet taste. Its ripe fruit hangs in bright clusters all over the garden.

The day came when we said goodbye and boarded the ferry back to Naples. We settled into a comfortable cabin, the horn sounded, and all seemed safe and happy. In short order we were faced with gigantic waves from the northwest, huge spray flying up as mare's tails. Our ferryboat shuddered, halted, lurched, rolled, and all I could imagine was that I would end up in Davy Jones's locker accompanied by Neptune. As my fear mounted, Fred slept peacefully. When we awoke to a safe harbor in Naples backed by the snowcapped Mount Vesuvius, it all seemed a dream.

If you go: Mondello Palace Hotel, Viale Principe di Scalea, 90151 Mondello Lido, Palermo, Sicily, Italy

Visiting Shops and Gardens
on Lake Como

THERE HAS ALWAYS BEEN SOMETHING ELUSIVE to me about summertime. I remember packing my bags for Camp Pinnacle when I was sixteen and stashing over ten novels into vacant corners in the suitcase. As we grow older, those days of summer fun, summer innocence, and summer leisure seem to disappear. We become immersed in our daily routines, our job requirements, and habit becomes our hallmark. Sometimes a fabulous summer vacation can bring you back to those pristine days of summer and youth. So it was for me one May day when we took off for a vacation on Lake Como, spending four nights in Hotel du Lac in Bellagio.

There is an Italian saying, "le mani d'angeli," that roughly translates to "the hands of angels," that gets to the heart of the Italian magic with handwork. Whether it is gold, glass, leather, silk, or a garden, the Italian has a sure and creative instinct with molding, shaping, and color. On the banks of Lake Como in the town of Bellagio, located where the three prongs of the lake come together, Italian handwork reigns supreme. The silk industry has long enjoyed prominence on Lake Como. Shops with exquisite silk scarves and silk bow ties are overflowing with tantalizing wares. Leather stores have stylish shoes, wallets and belts. Glass shops have hand-blown wineglasses and multicolored rings. Wood carving is a family endeavor that consumes the long, quiet days of the winter. Wood shops have everything from salad bowls to crèches. From shopping we returned to our lakeside hotel for dinner and sunset on the veranda.

The Italians call sunset *il tramonte del sole,* and indeed over Lake Como from Hotel du Lac, it was a spiritual experience. First, the lake turned pearl gray. As the setting sun touched puffy clouds, the entire sky was infused with pink. Finally, dark crept in, and sparkling lights brought expectations as does a twinkling Christmas tree. What presents awaited tomorrow? Asleep to dreams under a down comforter, I awakened to the expectation of one of the most marvelous of Italian gardens, Villa Carlotta.

The easiest transportation to Villa Carlotta is by ferryboat. We joined French, British, German, and Italian folk crossing the smooth waters of the lake to a dock at Villa Carlotta. Today the villa is owned by the Italian state. In mid-May the garden was aflame with azaleas and rhododendron planted in huge clumps of lavender, white, rose, and magenta. Lake Como was created by retreating glaciers, and the acidic soil nurtures acid-loving plants. The high walls of the Alps create a microclimate where rain and sun are plentiful and north winds are blocked. The result is a plethora of fabulous plants ranging from giant sequoias, huge feathery palms, bamboo groves, magnolias, splendid azaleas, and towering rhododendron. The garden at Villa Carlotta is an English-style park where landscape and vista intermingle to glorious effect. Villa Carlotta is also a magnificent small museum filled with ceramics, clocks, silver, and furniture. Each room features a marble statue by Canova or other famous Italian sculptors. The villa was built in the mid–seventeenth century by Giorgio Clerici, whose wealth was derived from the Como silk industry.

Villa Melzi with its sweeping gardens is just a ten-minute walk from Hotel du Lac in Bellagio, and the perfect destination for an early morning garden stroll. The garden and villa front the lake with a private dock. The entrance path leads through a serene Japanese garden where reflections of purple and red Japanese maples glimmer in a small pond. We meandered to a lakeside pavilion, the ideal spot to sit and watch white swans exploring the lake. The garden is an English-style pleasure park with outstanding trees including sequoias, tulip trees, white pines, red oaks, swamp cypresses, and Japanese maples. There are camphor trees and camellias, azaleas and rhododendron, all in full bloom. An eclectic variety of sculpture, including Egyptian and Roman sarcophagi and busts, guards the walks and frames the vistas over the lake.

That afternoon, we ventured on a private launch, across the glassy lake to Villa Balbianello, which sits on a promontory over Lake Como. Set in soaring woods of cypress, oak, and pollarded plane trees, Balbianello seemed enchanted. We climbed up the steep hillside where we could see all three branches of the lake. The villa, begun in 1787, is a perfect Italian summer casino. Each room has its blue and gray lake vista. We found a seat under the loggia between the library and music room, and we sat in the sun and breeze under the trellises, which are heavy with ficus vines.

Next morning we hiked up to Villa Serbelloni, owned today by the Rockefeller Foundation as a retreat for international study. The entrance to the villa lies on the square directly behind Hotel du Lac. We ambled up the steep path through woods that are filled with hornbeam, hazel, and holly trees. There we found carpets of Solomon's seal, lily of the valley, and hellebores in the glades. A thirty-minute hike uphill brought us to the highest point, with views toward the snowcapped mountains. Crews of gardeners were cutting spring grass and raking leaves.

A final Lake Como adventure was on a fast ferryboat for Varenna and Villa Monastero. The villa had its origins as a thirteenth-century Cistercian convent dedicated to Mary Magdalene. In the sixteenth century it was converted into a private home, and today it is a conference center. The garden is filled with exotic plants including palms, eucalyptus, tangerines, grapefruits, camphor trees, and agaves. The garden extends with terraces, fountains, pavilions, and loggias along the lake shore. We found a quiet seat and enjoyed watching the glint of the sun on the waves and the reflection of the mountains in the lake. Climbing yellow and pink

The fountain and stairway to Villa Carlotta, Lake Como, Italy

roses were interplanted with lavender clematis and cascade from arbors, Italian cypresses, and old stone walls. The perfume was heady. Finally, it was time to walk back to the ferry landing and catch the boat to Bellagio.

Saying goodbye to Lake Como was brightened by a visit to Villa d'Este, today a five-star resort with five-star luxury. The hotel fronts the lake with its own private dock. The public rooms are elegantly furnished, while many of the hotel rooms overlook the lake. The gardens, designed in the sixteenth century by Pellegrini, are extensive and beautifully manicured. A water cascade descends from the Hercules fountain, and a nymphaeum has bas-reliefs on the themes of solitude and love. Planted with Italian cypresses, the gardens retain much of their Renaissance design. Among the extras afforded the guests of Villa d'Este are clay tennis courts, an indoor pool and fitness center, and an outdoor infinity style swimming pool.

If you go: enjoying Lake Como requires advance planning. May is the top of the season, with six gardens (open May through end of October) for touring. There are ferryboats for cars should you want your own transportation or plan on visiting several locations. Ask for a room with a balcony on the lake at Hotel du Lac (www.bellagiohoteldulac.com; dulac@tin.it) or at the deluxe Grand Hotel Villa Serbelloni (www.villaserbelloni.com). Fly into Milan, rent a car, take the A 9 to Como, and the lake road to Bellagio. Stay at least four nights in Bellagio. Gardens worth visiting include Villa Carlotta (www.villacarlotta.it); Villa Melzi (Tel. 339 6446830, Fax 031 95318); Villa Balbinello (Tel. 0344 56110, Fax 0344 55575); Villa Serbelloni (Tel. 031 950204, Fax 031 951551); Villa Monastero (www.villamonastero.it); Villa d'Este (www.villadeste.it).

Italy

Gardening and Dining by the Sea

GARDENS BY THE SEA HAVE SPECIAL CHALLENGES. Wind, salt spray, sun, and aridity allow only the hardiest plants a chance to grow and flourish. Italy with its extensive coast line has a long history of gardens by the sea. On a recent trip we enjoyed four special gardens, all on seaside promontories. Each had a veranda for dining.

Gardens by the sea need protection from the wind. When storms arrive with black clouds, high shrill winds, and large waves, how best to protect one's garden investment? One seaside garden at Villa Tritone on the Gulf of Sorrento has an old and respected plan. It was here that Agrippa Postumus, a nephew of Augustus, built his home at sea level. When Vesuvius erupted in A.D. 79 a tsunami rolled over his seaside villa leaving it in ruins. Today, Villa Tritone and its garden sit on a high promontory above the original villa, overlooking the Bay of Naples. William Waldorf Astor purchased the land in the mid–nineteenth century. He built a new villa and constructed a twenty-foot gray stone, mullioned wall around the entire bay side of the garden. Elegant small windows with Renaissance style columns punctuate the wall. Doors onto seaside verandas provide vistas of a sparkling sea. In winter the windows have huge steel shutters that keep out the fiercest wind. Inside these cloistered walls Rita and Mariano Pane have created an oasis away from sea gales and sea salt. The Panes have preserved archaeological relics from the Roman villa and incorporated them as focal points in the garden. A stone siren sits serenely in

Rita Pane in her garden, Villa Tritone, on the Gulf of Sorrento

The LeClercqs having tea at Hotel Splendido, Portofino, Italy

The vista from La Cervara on the Ligurian Sea, Italy

one three-arched window enjoying her view of Vesuvius. Stone images of Mercury, Dionysus, Jupiter, Juno, and Mars adorn ancient columns. We joined Rita Pane on the terrace of Villa Tritone and enjoyed her stories about writing *Southern Italian Cooking.*

Gardens by the sea need shade from the hot and drying sun. La Cervara in Santa Margherita Ligure sits on a marvelous promontory overlooking the Mediterranean Sea. La Cervara began its life in 1364 as a monastery for the Benedictine Order. Today, the monastery and garden have been restored by Enrico Mapelli. La Cervara has extensive pergolas, covered with grape vines, wisteria, bougainvillea, and jasmine. We sat at a table, enjoyed the sea vista, and drank mint-flavored tea. The sea was alternately green or blue depending on whether white or gray clouds were overhead. The sound of birdsong filled the air as swallows and gulls soared on the ocean updrafts. We listened to the tinkling of water from the formal garden where box topiaries in geometrical cones surround a seventeenth-century marble fountain. La Cervara with its garden, ancient church, and great house is used today for celebratory occasions, special musical events, and weddings.

Gardening in pots and containers provides one method that a seaside gardener can use to create a protected microenvironment. Just five minutes from La Cervara at Portofino, we visited the magnificent Hotel Splendido. The garden is full of colorful flower-filled pots, and pots are replaced every Monday. When we were there, we found white asters with blue hydrangeas, pots of pink roses, and tubs full of orange and pink hibiscus. The hillside view to the Ligurian Sea, was verdant with mounded pines, silver olive trees, date palms with waving fronds, and tall pointing cypresses. Hotel Splendido, once a convent and converted into a luxury hotel by Orient Express, is tucked within this magical hillside. The vista of the sea that day was of an international navy of sailboats and motorboats waving flags of France, the United States, England, Greece, Italy, and many other nations. We sat in the shade under a pergola bright with purple bougainvillea and enjoyed hot tea, then moved to a table on the terrace overlooking the harbor for lunch. We began with a warm sea bass salad topped with cherry tomatoes, and then we dined on lamb loin "sanguine" with a sweet mint sauce accompanied by potatoes, onions, and zucchini. The lovely porcelain china with a green and pink border and the vase of yellow roses added a touch of elegance.

Once you have taken care of sun and wind, the greatest remaining challenge is water and the proper selection of plants. On the island of Ischia, La Mortella, whose name means myrtle, is the epitome of the perfectly planted garden. It contains more than eight hundred species of rare plants. Lady Susana Walton, the second wife of the famous British composer Sir William Walton, came with her husband in the 1950s to Ischia, and she began a garden by the sea. She brought in Russell Page, the famous British landscape designer, to help craft her garden. Page laid out a garden on multiple levels full of water in rills, ponds, fountains, and pools. Having

The waterfall at La Mortella on the island of Ischia, Italy

found a way to preserve water, Susana Walton began to plant. She brought seeds for the water lily Victoria Amazonica. This perfect water lily can be found floating, with its white and pink gigantic flowers, on two ponds. Another pond, just below an oriental garden house, has lotus flowers in bloom. Susana Walton loved hummingbirds. She told us that the Aztecs admired the hummingbird and hoped to return to life in its form as a fierce hummer. Two small glass houses with water fountains shelter her orchids. Every imaginable orchid was in bloom in colors of yellow, pink, purple, green. Outside of these protected ponds and glass houses, Lady Walton had planted specimen date palms and olive trees. Under the shade created by these plants are wonderful Australian tree ferns. La Mortella had been a dry and barren riverbed full of volcanic rocks thrown off by Epomeo, a volcano that rises over three thousand feet in the middle of Ischia. The stones still form a valuable and essential part of the garden, creating unusual focal points. We took the ferry-boat back to Naples, knowing that we had seen a unique garden.

I returned to my own garden by the sea in Charleston with the knowledge that by selecting the right plants, finding a protected location for them, and creating micro-environments away from wind and sun, it might be possible to create ones' own Italian garden by the sea.

If you go: www.villatritone.it; www.cervara.it; www.hotelsplendido.com; www.lamortella.it

Discovering Lucca,
an Italian Walled City

PLAIN BLACK SHOES JUST DO NOT DO IT in Lucca, Italy. Everywhere I looked there were stylish Italian ladies in pink silk shirts and pink leather walking shoes, or green turtlenecks and green high-heels. Long ago my son, Ben LeClercq, advised me to spare the white tennis shoes in Paris or be identified immediately as an American, *sans gout.*

We arrived on Monday, April 25; the quiet and peace in Lucca, following the Festival of Santa Zita, was an amazing contrast to the activity of the festival. The festival had brought throngs of Italians to the Square of San Frediano, a bright triangle of flowers and people in front of the eleventh-century church of San Zita. The golden and blue mosaic of Christ dominates the square. The Orto Botanico had provided an "instant garden," exquisitely planned with a towering twelve-foot-high potted rhododendron with crimson blooms.

Our hotel, the Ilaria, provides bicycles. Each morning we took the three-mile ride around the walls of the city. Lucca is surrounded by seventeenth-century brick fortifications that are thirty-seven feet high and fifty-five feet wide. The top of the wall forms a verdant garden, shaded by huge sycamore and plane trees, and it serves as the gathering place for the entire community.

Beautiful girls stroll their prancing yellow Labs or feisty Jack Russell terriers. The dogs greet and sniff while the mistresses chat and gossip. Men gather in groups to talk about sports, family, politics, and other issues of interest. Most of the ninety-seven Luchesi churches and many of the town's other ancient buildings can be seen from the wall. Italian men seem comfortable in orange trousers and orange leather shoes, or yellow trousers, or even light green trousers. Every Lucca mother is pushing a stroller with a new baby. The Italians claim that their population rate is 1 percent, but the hordes of babies evident on the parapets belie that claim. There are Boy and Girl Scout troops laughing and tweaking each other, while from the soccer stadium in the distance, the chanting and singing resonates in our ears.

Lucca is a friendly and ancient town that is entirely comfortable. It is a good base for trips to Florence, Pisa, and Volterra. We visited Florence to see the magnificent Vasari murals at the Palazzo Vecchio. Another day we journeyed over the verdant green hills to Volterra, an ancient Etruscan city built, as were most former Etruscan cities, on high hills, easily fortified by thick stone walls. Dominated by the towering Medici castle, the town is always windy and cold. Its delicate, transparent alabaster sculptures have been popular for generations. We visited artists' studios and workshops, enjoying the four true colors of alabaster: white, ochre, brown, and gray. The beautiful and transparent stone has been carved into charging horses, raging lions, and classic statues.

One day I climbed two of Lucca's towers. The view from the tree-topped Tower of the Guinigi provides a perspective of orange tiled roofs and small "snakes" of streets. I was puffing when I reached the top of the Torre del Oro and was soon deafened by the ringing of the bells of the tower clock. Lucca is a city of chiaroscuro, a city characterized by light and dark, like a painting of Caravaggio. I walked along the narrow stone streets, always to a new square that punctuated the dark of the street with bright light and activity. The Piazza Maria is dominated by its twelfth-century Duomo, while the Piazza Municipale is dominated by a huge bank and the Piazza San Michele by a thirteenth-century church clad in shining white marble, itself dominated by a statue of the saint. Near this square is an enigmatic bronze statue of Puccini, seated and smoking a cigar. Behind the statue at 3 Via della Cervia is the Buca di Sant'Antonio, Lucca's finest restaurant. We dined on trout from the nearby mountains of the Garfagnana and succulent lamb cutlets. The collection of old copper pots, gathered from ancient Lucca by the owner, Signor Franco, glint and reflect the happy throngs of Italian diners.

Amid this bustle and clatter it is possible to steal away for an hour and enjoy one of Lucca's lovely formal gardens, such as that at the Palazzo Pfanner. The garden was blooming with wisteria, whose sweet aroma was amplified by the scent of lilacs in bloom. An assortment of oranges and lemons in old clay pots surround a central fountain. I wandered by myself enjoying the high-pitched staccato singing of a chorus of birds.

Villa Torrigiani is a perfectly maintained garden a short distance from Lucca. It has been owned by the same family since 1730. It was built in 1500 as a summer residence by the powerful Buonvisi family of Lucca, one of whom was the Luchesi ambassador to the French court of Louis XIV. The garden of the estate was designed by the French architect André Le Nôtre. The two symmetrical water pools designed by Le Nôtre in front of the Baroque mansion provide reflections of the highly decorated villa. Once a classical Italian Renaissance garden, today only the secret garden retains the hallmarks of classic design: water and plant parterres, elegant staircases with balustrades, grottoes, and graceful marble statues as focal points. On a February visit the garden anticipated spring. Blue and pink hydrangeas had been carefully pruned to maximize summer blooms. Camellias had thousands of bursting buds. Yellow and blue pansies had been set out in all of the parterres. Pergolas showed the lacy bare stems of budding wisteria. On the wide lawns there were specimen magnolias, clipped in conical form. Enormous gray plane trees, magnificent tulip poplars, and huge elms and gums were carefully spaced on the vast lawn to give a parklike effect. Villa Torrigiani, also known as Villa di

Palazzo Pfanna, Lucca, Italy

Camigliano, is a perfect destination for a picnic, away from the hustle and bustle of Lucca.

Travel can be tiresome: the fatigue of jet lag, the different routines, the exotic food, the feeling of being out of one's own routine. This is also what makes it exciting and challenging. The charm of Lucca is its human scale. The crowds are local. Masses of tourists, such as one finds in Florence or Rome, are nonexistent. Wandering by oneself is safe and gives a sense of discovery and adventure. I always know that if I get lost in Lucca, I can head for the walls and within five minutes find my way back to headquarters, the Hotel Ilaria.

If you go: Hotel Ilaria (Tel. 0583 47615); Buca di san Antonio (Tel. 0583 55881)

Ninfa

A Romantic Italian Garden

SOUTH OF ROME AND NORTH OF NAPLES, the garden of Ninfa is situated below the escarpment of Norma and the Lepini Mountains. It has been described as a Medieval Pompeii. The garden was laid out in the 1920s among the ruins of the small medieval town of Ninfa founded in the eighth century. Today, with an abundance of spring-fed water and a salubrious microclimate, the garden flourishes in the middle of vast vineyards and olive orchards.

The garden is rich in color with more than twelve thousand flowering shrubs, trees, bulbs, and water plants. Pinks, yellows, iridescent greens, bronzes, deep roses, blues, and grays please the eye with a rainbow palette. On one of the days that we visited, the spring-fed river of Ninfa reflected the aqua, blue, gray, and black of the sky as well as trailing vines of wisteria, clematis, and purple irises. There was a barrage of sweet birdsong from hundreds of species that make Ninfa their home. The wind harpies played in the huge towering pines, singing their songs. Finally, there were tempting smells of breath of spring, lavender, and roses. The garden is a veritable paradise to tempt all the senses and thus awaken a wonder at the bounty of nature.

Ninfa combines the ruins of an old and venerable medieval town with today's garden. The land has been owned by one family, the Caetini, for more than seven hundred years. Ninfa began in the 700s as a small crossroads located on the Apian way, between Naples and Rome. It became the fiefdom of the popes. The land was acquired by Pietro Caetini in 1297 for 200,000 gold florins. The town flourished under the Caetinis with 2,000 inhabitants, 150 houses, gardens, fields, a castle with a double-walled enclosure, and seven churches. Ninfa was sacked in 1381 by mercenary troops from Brittany, and its inhabitants fled to Sermoneta. The village was abandoned, forgotten, and crumbled into a maze of walls and fallen church apses covered by vines and trees.

In the 1920s Gelasio Caetani and his wife, Ada, who still held the land for the Caetani family, began the restoration of the area within the old walls. Gelasio was an architect and had restored the castle that surmounts Sermoneta. He knew the methods for bringing old brick, stones, and mortar to life. Ada planted the old streets with alleys of towering cypresses and cedars. She also ensured there was an abundance of flowering shrubs and trees: apples, magnolias, and peaches. Gelasio restored the dam on the lake and strengthened the five bridges over the Ninfa River.

The tower at Ninfa, near Latina, Italy

Into the clear white waters of the river, Gelasio introduced African trout. The old and forgotten ruin was once again alive with the sound of human voices.

Ada's sister-in-law, Marguerite Caetani, inherited the garden. Her specialty was camellias, roses, and maples whose bronze, yellow, and green leaves were to give the garden a fall perspective. With her husband, Roffredo, she designed distinctive watercourses that are richly planted with irises and a bamboo grove. After World War II the estate passed to Lelia Caetani, who had married Hubert Howard. Lelia was an artist, and her palette created the color, form, and continuity throughout the seasons that make Ninfa a garden for each day of the year.

Ninfa is a romantic garden. Each turn of a path surprises with another ruin or towering tree or flowering shrub. Only by wandering the paths among the ruins does one discover the abundance of color, form, and shape. Such surprises are the antithesis of a classic garden where one is led by geometric paths to ultimate focal points. There is no one focal point, but a plethora of changing shapes as plants and ruins intermingle. The garden is a garden of moods, with its central life the singing river Ninfa. Wherever one walks, there are vistas that include the yellow, pink, and ochre tower of the castle, the green and blue escarpment of the surrounding mountains, the aqua blue of the firmament, and the abundant, intense green of the plants intertwined with the old ruins.

If you go: Hotel Principe Serrone, via Del Serrone, Sermoneta, Italia (Tel. 0773 30342 or 30343, Fax 0773 30336); hotel.serrone@virgilio.it. Ninfa is open on the first weekend of every month from April through October. Groups can have special tours by contacting the following: La Direzione, Giardini di Ninfa, 04010 Doganella di Ninfa, Latina, Italy (Tel. 07 73 69 54 04).

The Amalfi Coast

Positano, Ravello, and Capri

I RECALL SO VIVIDLY SITTING IN POSITANO on a promontory under a lemon-scented arbor, and watching a luminous pink and gray Mediterranean ocean. The air was scented with jessamine and orange blossoms, while my eyes were bedazzled by the red and violet hues of bougainvillea and geraniums. The lulling sounds of Italian soothed my ears, while low humidity and chilly nights let spring linger pleasantly into summer.

Our mistaken apprehension over a possible crime-ridden southern Italy had kept us in Tuscany and Umbria. Yet family tales of the golden era of travel to Naples and Sorrento tempted us. Our base in southern Italy was Positano, and our rented villa was Villa Fiorita, the winter home of Signor Donato of Arrezzo. The villa is up twenty-five steps from the street, with terraces under lemon arbors. That night as a full red moon rose to the south and east, we celebrated our good fortune at being on the Amalfi coast.

Our first adventure was Pompeii. Mount Vesuvius was ringed in clouds that ignited my imagination. Pompeii amazed by its solid mass. Some twenty thousand citizens had lived compactly and in close proximity with cultural and governmental institutions intermixed at easy reach from villas and dwelling houses. The sense of spirituality was evident in small altars where the household gods protected the family enclosure. Gardens with central fountains spoke to the importance of privacy and beauty.

We enjoyed preparing the evening meal at our villa overlooking the sea. Fresh salmon and bass were steeped in herbs and lemon, while local zucchini and tomatoes were topped with mozzarella. Another evening we dined on spaghetti bolognese, while another it was chicken cacciatore. Ernesto, the purveyor at the local grocery, had abundant, well-stocked shelves.

We were delighted by the elegance of Positano. Hanging over cliffs, its sheer verticality became quickly apparent the next morning as I ran down to the sea for a morning swim. I counted eight hundred steps and quit. I plunged headlong into the aqua, cold sea, letting out a squeal of delight. I looked down to boulders below as I swam out to moored sailboats. I stopped my ears against mermaids and monsters of the deep that beckoned me into their watery caverns. The beach was a maze of fine pebbles, uncomfortable to tender toes.

The next morning we set off by high-speed boat to Capri. An international crowd made it a lively journey across the sea with German, French, Italian, and English speech happily intermingling. We joined a French hiking group and toiled our way up to Villa San Michaele at Ana Capri. Our walk led directly to the marvelous villa, the famed home of Axel Munthe, a Swedish doctor. The whitewashed villa is set in gardens whose arbors incorporate columns from Roman ruins. Roman bronzes and marbles made stunning focal points starkly set against the vista of the sea. Moss and maidenhair ferns bespoke the presence of water. A small rill sung its hymn through the garden. We nestled into a curving marble seat three thousand feet above the Mediterranean and toasted to the spirits of Hadrian and Augustus. Leaving the villa, we caught an open air taxi and found a quiet beach in Piccola Marina. We changed into bathing suits and swam out through a grotto into the blue-green waters of a perfect bay.

I wondered if each day could be so entrancing, and indeed they were. We took out next morning for Sorrento and Palazzo Correale museum. At one point at the top of the way, we could see back to Positano and the Salerno Gulf and in the other direction the Gulf of Naples with Sorrento. The Correale museum offers four stunning floors of fine art. Pink, green, and blue Chinese urns grace exquisite inlaid commodes. Meissen figurines and Venetian glass adorn marble mantles. A fine collection of nineteenth century landscapes tell of an earlier, less complicated world. We dined on the piazza of the Victoria Royal Excelsior Hotel. We delighted in the stunning view of Vesuvius and an ever-changing sea and sky. Sorrento is known for its fine woodworking with exquisitely detailed intaglio.

That evening in Positano our destination was the restaurant Le Sirenuse. The view was spectacular. The green and yellow tiled dome of the cathedral echoed the green and yellow of a lemon tree. White linens on the table, with four or five waiters hovering in attendance, set the style. A ten-pronged table candelabra with votive candles cast shadows. Dinner arrived slowly. My spouse's appetizer was steamed clams and mussels and little shrimp served with long beans. The mixed green salad had just the proper blend of oil and balsamic vinegar. White and red local wine spurred conversation. We treated ourselves to lamb chops, exquisitely presented with bones making a triangular crown, and a pungent prune sauce with oranges glazed the succulent meat. A mixed berry sherbet, light and pure in fruit taste, charmed our finale. On the wall of Le Sirenuse is the memorable Steinbeck quote: "Positano bites deep. It is a dream place that isn't quite real when you are there and becomes beckoningly real after you have gone."

Next morning we took the famed Amalfi drive to Ravello. The trip is sixteen kilometers of nail-bitingly steep uphill hairpin curves to Ravello which is perched on a limestone mountain precipice high above the Tyrrhenian Sea. The vista from the clifftop promentory at Villa Cimbrone is unique, awesome. The village is dominated by the monastery (San Francisco) and by two very old villas, Villa Cimbrone and Villa Rufolo. Their fabulous Italian gardens were our destination. Cimbrone, a classical garden, has a grand bronze of David with the head of Goliath framed in a vista of umbrella pines. A rose garden held my attention with its "all at once" design and a central marble urn as a focal point. A long avenue led to the belvedere with its Roman temple, colossal marble maiden, and unparalleled view. The garden at Rufolo was intimate in contrast. Rufolo is a villa built on the ruins of an earlier structure. The old arches and pillars accented the garden. We went up through a series of passageways to a small terrace. We could see for miles over the Mediterranean. A few steps led to a larger terrace with a formal garden filled with workers planting geraniums and begonias. We walked to the edge of the precipice, looking over the small village, to the sea below. As I stood in silence, the colors of the ocean changed from emerald green to blue to various shades of gray-blue. Renting a private villa in Positano provided us a perfect base for enjoying the history, beauty, and charm of the Amalfi coast.

If you go:
Le Sirenuse, Via Cristoforo Colombo, 30–84017 Positano, Italy, info@sirenuse.it (Tel. 39 089 875066)

Hotel Luna Convento, Amalfi, www.lunahotel.it, originally a convent found by St. Francis of Assisi. The central cortile is well preserved. A fine restaurant and luxurious suites with cliff vistas over the sea

Imperial Hotel Tramontano, www.hoteltramontano.it, on a bluff at Sorrento, an elegant hotel set in a lovely garden. The sunset from the balcony of our suite over the Bay of Naples and the profile of Mount Vesuvius will forever linger in our memories.

Grand hotel Excelsior Vittoria, www.exvitt.it, a sublime garden at the entry of this luxury hotel on the high bluff at Sorrento. The terrace features ancient marble busts and incomparable views from the bar and restaurant.

Italian Renaissance Gardens

A Day Trip from Rome

I INHERITED A LOVE FOR ITALIANATE GARDENS from my great-aunt Emily Roosevelt, whose garden at Gippy Plantation, in Berkeley County, South Carolina, had all the elements of an Italian garden. Emily had traveled in Italy and brought back graceful urns and dignified marble statues of Mercury, Diana, and Venus. With these ornaments she created the perfect Italian garden. Her long paths of crushed seashells ended with a focal point, usually a statue that stopped and captured the eye. Her pergolas provided seating nooks. Her watercourses, pools, and fountains brought the sounds of water into the midst of the garden.

Five Italian gardens, each a day trip from Rome, epitomize the Italian style. In describing each the focus will be on two key features: the lay of the hilly land and how the architect used this to create a garden; and how architectural ornaments, including staircases, balustrades, gates, fountains, urns, and buildings, are used to focus the eye, define space, and create a gray and green palette for the year-round garden.

Villa Lante dates to the 1560s, when Cardinal Gianfrancesco Gambara hired architect Giacomo Barozzi da Vignola to create this Renaissance garden. The garden is entered through twin villas that were used as summer entertainment pavilions for the popes. Vignola used a variety of techniques to create a geometric garden within an ascending rectangular space. This classic Italianate garden is organized on four different levels along a main axis with a sequence of fountains on each level. The fountains were completed by Carlo Maderno in 1612. The garden has perfect symmetry.

At the entry there are the twin villas overlooking twelve geometric parterres, eight of which are filled with clipped boxwood, and four of which are blue reflecting pools. Statues of four naked men form the central fountain holding aloft the cardinal's insignia. From here the garden ascends through three levels of cascading water fountains to a grotto. Descending from the grotto, the first fountain is the fountain of the deluge. Here the water is gurgling, singing, and pounding. We smelled the pungent scent of boxwood, ilex, and laurel. Another level down is the fountain of the dolphins, an octagonal fountain representing the water of the sea. White water cascades down a precipitous water staircase into the fountain of the giants, representing the two rivers, the Arno and the Tiber. Water is the heart and soul of this garden, and its four blue-water parterres throw back the undimmed azure of the Italian sky. Water explodes from the wilderness represented by grottoes and is transformed and tamed through fountains. This is also a garden of stone and evergreen plants. Huge plane trees, without their leaves in December, form a

A river god at Villa Lante, Bagnaia, Italy

lacework of branches against the sky. Each level has a green backdrop of clipped boxwood hedges, backed by azaleas and rhododendron. This is perhaps my favorite Italian garden, and whenever we are near Bagnaia, we stop in to savor its beauty.

Sacro Bosco, nine miles from Viterbo and a day trip from Rome, is at Bomarzo. The garden was created by Vicino Orsini beginning in 1552 and is a setting for giant stone beasts. It is a garden of wild imagination. Orsini was steeped in classical mythology, myths that tell of the dark and dangerous side of the world and how the brave slay dragons. This bizarre and dark matter from ancient literature is the source of the monumental stone creations in the thickly forested garden of Sacro Bosco. There are enormous stone sculptures covered with green moss and ferns. Light filters through the bare branches of deciduous trees, giving remarkable clarity to these creatures. Cerberus, the three-headed dog, guards the entrance to Hades. According to legend at least one of the heads was awake all of the time. A small classically designed temple sits elegantly in its glade. A winged dragon is eating a leopard, while a serene, classic lady seems undisturbed nearby. A river god is swathed in moss, and a sensuous nude entices. The monstrous open-mouthed fish is like the whale that swallowed Jonah. The huge grotto into the ground represents crossing the Styx and going into the underground, where Pluto took Persephone. Sacro Bosco is a place of imagination, of myth, of fables, of nymphs, and of fairies. It can excite the fears and imagination of grown-ups as well as children.

Villa d'Este is in Tivoli, a short train or car ride just twenty miles east of Rome. On a snowy February day we had this amazing garden all to ourselves. Pirro Ligorio was commissioned in 1550 by Cardinal Ippolito d'Este to design both house and garden. This is an architectural and sculptural garden of the High Renaissance, with a central plunging axis that goes down five levels and is crossed by a horizontal axis. Its wonders are discovered by paths of white marble and black granite set in geometric mosaics. Stairs and paths lead between each level where clipped boxwood and laurels, oval firs, and cylindrical cedars with glistening cones provide a dark green backdrop. The garden has a spectacular display of white water—gushing, spouting, cascading, and finally still and reflecting in square water parterres. There are wonderful fountains: the Ephesian Diana with her multiple breasts; the cascading water fountain with the water parterres below; the avenue of one hundred fountains with sprays and jets, some coming from the mouths of animals; and the Rometta Fountain with Romulus and Remus. This is a garden whose sounds are those of water, whose vistas are the blue and gray sky and distant mountains, whose trees and shrubs are glistening green, and whose paths are like the yellow-brick road leading to multiple wonders.

Nearby, also in Tivoli, is Hadrian's Villa Adriana. It is an enormous complex of gardens and buildings constructed in a.d. 118 by Emperor Hadrian (Publius Aelius Hadrianus). He designed Villa Adriana to incorporate the sights he had seen in Egypt, Syria, Spain, and France during his many travels throughout his empire. It was to become his summer home. The complex is on the Aniene River and covers over 300 acres. Important to a garden lover is the fact that the complex comprises buildings that are complemented by gardens and open spaces that include fountains as well as lakes surrounded by statues. The villa was originally covered with fabulous marble of all colors and types, and it is known that more than five hundred marble statues have been removed and are in museums. We see today what remains after two thousand years, and it has inspired landscape architects since its rediscovery during the Renaissance.

The Canopus area is a long pool that recalls the canal that led from Alexandria to Canopus, a town on the Nile delta. It was used for outdoor dining and is surrounded with freestanding, columned walls interspersed with statues. The large and small bathing complex had many chambers for hot and cold baths. There is a classic temple to Venus, and nearby one finds an area where Hadrian met with dignitaries from the empire. Rosy brick walls provide protection for aquatic plants and life and enclose the Pecile, a large pool that served as an area for exercise and walks during Hadrian's time. Seeing these fantastic remains excited my imagination and inspired me to read more about Rome.

Going southeast from Rome, we find Villa Aldobrandini, which dominates the town of Frascati. An imposing wall with iron grates encloses the vast estate. The

Villa d'Este and the walk of a hundred fountains, Tivoli, Italy

sun comes across the villa and its gardens from the east to the west. The garden and the villa were built by Cardinal Pietro Aldobrandini in 1598. The entry is dominated by the fountain of Atlas, who holds a watery ball representing the Earth on his shoulders. This classic water theater is framed by a wall ornamented with pilasters and niches with grand statues. At the side of Atlas are sculptures of Polyphemus playing the pipes and a centaur playing his horn. A small, secret garden to the right of the water fountain is thickly planted with camellias and hydrangeas surrounding huge old plane trees. On the terrace behind the Atlas fountain, there is a great runnel of water flowing from the top of the hill over a water staircase. It is enclosed by an alley of clipped holm oaks. In the woods on the top of the hill, a small grotto spouts water. This allegory of water from its natural to its controlled state echoes the similar theme from Villa Lante. Villa Aldobrandini and the town of Frascati provide a delightful country setting from which one can look back to the Seven Hills of Rome. The villa and its garden form an enormous enclosure that is chiaroscuro in effect. The dark of the woods contrasts sharply with the bright spaces of the courtyards, staircases, and the broad vista in the distance.

Each of the five Renaissance villas with their gardens is an easy day trip from Rome. However, staying overnight, whether in Viterbo, Tivoli, or Frascati, provided us a delightful destination away from the traffic and tourists of Rome.

Visiting Gardens near Florence

Villa Le Balze, Villa Gamberaia, Villa I Tatti, the Boboli Gardens, and La Pietra

THE BOBOLI GARDENS IN FLORENCE form a magnificent public space. Boboli is an old Italian word for forest. Begun in 1549 by Duke Cosimo de' Medici and his wife, Eleonora di Toledo, the garden is grand in scale and very much a part of the Pitti Palace. Entry through the Pitti Palace leads into a spreading amphitheatre dominated by venerable marble statues and fountains from ancient Rome. The design is by Tribolo, and work was begun in 1579.

The central axis has a splashing fountain of Neptune. Mallards were quacking in the pool below the fountain on the April day that we visited. Centered on the hill above is a huge marble of Ceres, the Goddess of Plenty, who holds aloft an abundance of wheat and fruit. A vine-covered pergola leads to the famed Bernardini secret garden, an area rarely found by tourists. It has vistas over Florence to snowcapped mountains. This is a gardener's garden. There are massive pots of azaleas and rhododendron and a small watercourse protected by a serpent. The hills of Florence provide a vantage point that makes the soul sing. Brunelleschi's Duomo is breathtaking in the vista from the garden's edge. As you leave the Boboli, there is a statue of a funny fat man on a turtle which marks the entrance to the classic grotto gardens.

A garden is an artificial creation. Perhaps the garden of Paradise had perfect gardening conditions. Since then, every gardener has faced the challenge of creating a garden under adverse conditions. We all know those curse words: deer, insects, wind, lack of water, too much sun, salt spray, earth that does not percolate, steep terrain. These conditions force creative gardeners to adapt, to change, to find horticultural specimens that will flourish. Despite adversity gardeners worldwide have devised solutions. Terraces provide wonderful garden rooms on steep terrain. Walls and hedges provide cover from wind. High shade trees, blocking the sun, create a welcoming environment for shade-loving plants. Cisterns, pools, and watering systems are the answer where aridity is the challenge. Many of the gardens of the Arno Valley reflect a skillful use of hilly terrain.

Brilliant vistas of the Arno Valley, the Duomo of Florence, and spreading olive orchards abound from the gardens of Fiesole, a small Tuscan town in the hills several miles north of Florence. We stayed several times in Pensione Bencistà, whose rambling, comfortable bedrooms with small balconies have lovely vistas over the hillside of olive groves and the city. The Bencistà gardens and wisteria-laden pergolas

Garden entrance, Villa
Le Balze, Fiesole, Italy

are special in early spring. We enjoyed Hotel Villa Aurora, and our fine balcony over its garden in the heart of the village of Fiesole just across the street from the Etrusco-Roman archaeological site. Hotel Villa San Michele is very special. It was once a convent, the façade of which is attributed to Michaelangelo. The garden and plantings are lovely. Their dining loggia is the best place for lunch in the area because of its splendid vista over the city of Florence. The restaurant is gourmet, and the service impeccable as we have found in every Orient Express hotel we have visited.

Tuscany is famous for its exquisite gardens despite its aridity, searing summers, bitter winters, and hilly terrain. One especially creative adaptation to those conditions is the garden at Villa Le Balze in Fiesole. Le Balze means "the Cliffs" in Italian, and this garden stretches along a precipice. Italians have learned to garden with three elements: stone, evergreens and water. At Le Balze, these elements are combined skillfully to create seven garden rooms connected by steps. This garden faces the special challenge of being on a long, narrow hillside perch. Cecil Pinsent,

(1884–1964) the British landscape architect, created this garden in 1912 for Charles Augustus Strong, an American philosopher. Pinsent created a series of narrow garden rooms connected by openings. He used windows onto the vista to frame views. His choice of evergreens included hardy plants such as boxwood, yew, ilex, privet, and cypresses. The garden is sited on the south facing the landscape of the Arno Valley to encompass that wider landscape within the garden. A wonderful glass house creates a hideaway during freezing months for lemons and orange trees, which are harbored there in pots. In summer these superb specimens are moved onto terraced formal gardens providing bright color and sweet scents. Herbs such as lavender and rosemary are used to edge the formal beds. Tulips planted in fall provide the perfect choice for color in spring. Owned today by Georgetown University, Le Balze shows superb creativity in using terraces, walls, garden sculpture, and evergreens to meet the unique challenges of a Tuscan garden.

We last visited the villa and garden of Villa I Tatti in early spring when a lush bed of red and white tulips shone above a bed of blue irises. The garden was the creation of Bernard Berenson, who lived here from 1900 to 1959. Today it is owned by Harvard University and has a wonderful art library. The garden is classic Italian Renaissance in style with a central axis of stairs leading down between topiaries and flower-filled parterres.

The formal garden at Villa I Tatti, near Fiesole, Italy

A view of the formal garden, Villa I Tatti, Italy

The celebrated 57 acre Renaissance revival garden, La Pietra, lies a mile outside the old Florence wall and is approached by a long, majestic avenue of ancient cypress trees. Our tour was led by Nicholas Dakin-Elliot, the director for reconstruction of the garden and its impressive collection of sculpture. The villa was bought in 1908 by Arthur Acton (1873–1953) and his wife, the Chicago banking heiress, Hortense Mitchell, whose fortune enabled Acton to buy the estate, its antiques and fabulous collections of art and more than 180 antique garden statuary. Their son, Harold, an important Oxford-trained scholar, bequeathed the estate in 1994 to New York University.

In his *Memoirs of an Aesthete* (1948) Harold Acton states that the Italian garden is a natural extension of the villa and that the villa and garden at La Pietra is developed on two perpendicular axes to provide lovely views from house and garden. The garden has impressive watercourses, terraces, walls, pergolas, and fountains. Outstanding views can be had of the Duomo and Florence skyline. The garden has

A temple of love at La Pietra, Florence, Italy

a theater en plain aire and is a center of graduate study which offers seminars on a wide range of subjects including professional gardening.

Close by in Settignano is Villa Gamberaia, which overlooks the olive orchards and countryside of the Arno River valley. The fifteenth-century villa overlooks a double water parterre that is backed by a semicircular hedge of clipped cypresses. A day trip into the hills of Florence can be made a country delight when one visits Le Balze, Villa I Tatti, La Pietra, and Villa Gamberaia.

If you go:
Hotel Villa Aurora, www.villaurora.net, Piazza Mino 39, Fiesole

info@bencista.com, Via Benedetto de Maiano, Fiesole

info@villasanmichele.com, Via Doccia 4, Fiesole

Be sure to take along Penelope Hobhouse's *The Garden Lover's Guide to Italy.*

Tuscan Gardens

Villa Chigi Cetinale and Villa La Foce

IN MAY THE SLOPES OF MT. AMIATA NEAR SIENA look like a checkerboard with patches of deep green fields beside the lighter green of newly mowed swathes of grass. White dirt roads, edged by black green cypress, snake up the hillsides, beckoning one to explore the unknown. Eight miles southwest of Siena, one such country road led to the gates of Villa Chigi Cetinale. Built in 1680 by Cardinal Flavio Chigi of the famous Siena banking family, Cetinale is a Baroque-style villa. Carlo Fontana (1634–1714), a pupil of Bernini, designed this classic villa. The villa and garden have been meticulously restored by the late Lord Lambton, a minister in Edward Heath's Tory government.

The villa lies on an east-west axis, with a geometric Italian style garden on the east side and a cypress-lined avenue on the west extending to a hermitage on the hill. The villa is purposefully sited so that the view of the rolling blue and green hills is part of the overall visual impact. An English garden full of roses, irises, peonies, and lilacs lies just to the south of the villa. On the day we visited, the wisteria and roses were in bloom, perfuming the air delicately. Pergolas and covered archways were covered with hundreds of climbing roses in shades of yellow, pink, crimson, and white.

We stopped to talk with Fernando, the handsome Italian gardener, who was busily pruning the lemons. I asked him how he had managed to produce such heavily fruited specimens. He said, in flavorful Italian that it was all *spulo* (fertilizer). His maxim was to fertilize with an organic mix in February and March and then prune carefully after fruiting in May. The results were stunning with huge lemon trees in large clay pots, covered with fat yellow fruit.

We left Fernando and took the hike up two hundred steps to the five-story hermitage, which the architect Fontana had completed in 1713. Today it is restored, and the view of the Tuscan hills from the skyline makes the climb worthwhile. We walked more easily back down through a cypress-lined avenue. Long slender afternoon shadows were making a strong diagonal pattern along the ground between the soaring cypresses that form this striking avenue.

Thankful for the lengthening daylight of May, we took a back road to Montepulciano and Villa La Foce. We had first learned of Villa la Foce from our friend Morna Livingston's wonderful photographs for Benedetta Origo's book *La Foce: A Garden and Landscape in Tuscany.* Villa La Foce was restored by Marchesa Origo (the writer Iris Origo). The marchesa and her husband had purchased the derelict

Villa Chigi Cetinale, near Siena, in Tuscany, Italy

Looking west from Chigi Cetinale toward the hermitage, Tuscany, Italy

farmhouse in the 1920s and planted a lovely garden. The garden was designed as a classic Italian style garden by the English architect Cecil Pinsent. He designed multiple garden rooms. The first room was highly geometric with wide box hedges enclosing green swathes of grass. Bright pink peonies were blooming. A wisteria arbor was redolent with scent and the sound of bees. There were green lizards sunning themselves or scampering away from under foot. We reached the terrace with its superb view of Mt. Amiata and watched as the sun spread its wings and headed west. We could hear the wind in the tall cypresses and listened for the sound of the night owl. Now the sun had set. We were no longer in a garden under the Tuscan sun.

On another trip, we headed back to Siena for the night. Our hotel, Alma Domus, is an ancient nunnery that had an exquisite view of the Cathedral of Saint Catherine. My husband, on making the reservation, had said, "We only want a view of the cathedral." Upon entry, the sister said, "Signor LeClercq, we have your room." He said, "But does it have a view?" And she responded, "Well, it has two beds." And yet our wondering eyes, on our entrance into a simple room, found that the entire cathedral, brilliantly illuminated, dominated the view off our small balcony. What a delightful and unexpected surprise. We woke up the next morning, opened the shutters, and found the entire panorama covered with an inch or two of snow.

If you go:

Alma Domus, run by the sisters, on Via Camporegio 37, in Siena
(Fax 0577 476 01)

Both gardens are open by appointment: Villa La Foce (Tel. 0578 69101); Villa Chigi Cetinale (Tel. 0577 311147, Fax 0577 311061)

The vista from Villa La Foce, near Siena, Italy

A Tale of Two Cities

Taormina and Venice

SEVERAL YEARS AGO, WHILE VISITING MY SON Kershaw LeClercq at the Leysin School in Switzerland, I discovered why my suitcase was unexpectedly heavy—my mother, Emily Whaley, had selected several small marble stones from a roadway for the stream in her "secret" garden in Charleston and stuffed them in my suitcase! Now, while we were at the Greek Theater in Taormina, Sicily, I turned to find my husband, Fred, marveling at the massive columns of pink and white marble from a 300 B.C. Greek theater. And, oh, what a setting for a theater! On a spit of land over the Strait of Messina, the Greeks built a massive theater that still echoes their tales of glory. A glistening, snowcapped Mt. Etna towers over the proscenium. Taormina sits in lovely countryside where vineyards and silvery olive orchards predominate. Our base was the Timeo Hotel overlooking the public gardens, the "dream" garden of a Scottish sweetheart of Edward VII. The garden is filled with brick and marble follies. A dramatic belvedere provides a promenade overlooking the sea. On our visit the park was resplendent with sago, canary, and date palms. Groves of sweet-smelling oranges and limes provided winter color to an otherwise green landscape.

Taormina bustles with the activity and sounds of a small village. Saturday produced two flower-filled weddings, or *nozze,* as the Italians call them. We were onlookers at a wedding reception at the Hotel Santa Dominica, an old monastery converted into an elegant hotel. We sat in the formal garden, overlooking the sea, and drank in the panoramic vista. Circular parterres were defined by rosemary, rather than by boxwood, and enclosed colorful circles of birds of paradise. As the sun set, the aqua ocean became an opalescent reflection of the pink and lavender sky. We slowly returned to the Timeo enjoying the *passagata,* the Italian evening stroll. Each evening we listened to the lively piano music of Salvatore Pennisi, whose forte is American jazz, including such tunes as "Unforgettable," "Fly Me to the Moon," and "In the Mood." Italians have a love affair with American culture, and they readily welcome and accept Americans and the English language.

We left the countryside of Sicily, flying out of Catania, for the bustling energy of Venice. Venice is a city where one should walk until completely lost and then discover the way back. The canals, alleys, and byways that link the many sunny *campos* (city squares) of Venice provide the routes for this discovery and exploration. The fun is in the exploration. Getting lost leads to wonderful conversations with locals, all too happy to help you find the way. Our base was the centrally located

Mt. Etna and the Greek amphitheater at Taormina

Gritti Palace, which overlooks the Grand Canal. We decided to explore Venice pursuing two themes, images of Mary Magdalene and images of St. George slaying the dragon. We found the beautiful and heartbroken Mary Magdalene with her pot of ointment (spikenard, the aromatic oil that she used to anoint the feet of Jesus) in the School of San Rocco, a huge Renaissance building with more than seventy gigantic paintings by Tintoretto (1518–1594). An enormous crucifix painting dramatically tells the story of Good Friday. There at the foot of the cross is Mary Magdalene, an image of grief and beauty. We found Mary again at the Campo dei Frari. The *campo* was a lively scene of barking dogs, flower and food vendors, and couples walking arm in arm. The Frari is an enormous church whose central altarpiece features a Titian ascension of the Virgin. But it was again a crucifix scene, this time by Bellini, that brought tears to my eyes. Two bas-relief marble scenes on either side of the altar piece showed Mary holding up her pot of ointment (said to be worth ten thousand dollars today) to the feet of a still-living Christ.

Finally, we had enough of grief, art, and history, and we sought a wonderful garden restaurant, the Locanda Montin. There under the wisteria vines of a shade-filled garden, we had a dinner of scaloppini with asparagus and *filetto di bue* (beef), which was suitably rare.

Now it was time to find St. George and his fire-eating dragon. We wended our way beyond San Zaccaria, an exquisite marble fronted church, and down Rio de Greci. There a handsome Italian in bright yellow pants advised that we were close to our destination, the School of San Giorgio degli Schiavoni. Just over the next bridge in a tiny gallery, we found three dramatic paintings by Vittore Carpaccio, telling the story of St. George and his slaying of the dragon. Legend has it that the people of a small Italian town were being devoured by a fearsome dragon; and indeed in the first painting their gruesome remains litter the ground. St. George, clad in black amour, is charging the dragon and using his huge lance to wrench out its blood and guts. The details of the scene are stunning: pieces of legs, heads, live lizards, and in the foreground a desperate heroine praying for the dragon's demise. The dragon reminded me of the alligators that line the banks of our own Charleston County park, Caw Caw. The details of the paintings, the dogs, the parrot, and the beautiful princess surprise and astonish.

The delights of Venice were many and included the sunlit *campos,* the friendly and welcoming Italians, and the happy gondoliers. Yes, we did take the requisite gondola ride, but down a byway where we enjoyed peeking into courtyards and windows. Our gondolier, Marco, was a charmer in his black and white shirt and with his wide-brimmed straw hat.

If you go:
Grand Hotel Timeo, Taormina, Sicily, info@hoteltimeo.net,
www.sandomenicopalace.hotelsinsicily.it

Gritti Palace Hotel, Venice, Italy, www.grittipalace.com,
grittipalace@starwoodhotels.com

Part 3

Switzerland

THE ART OF SEASONAL GARDENING

discovered Switzerland through the American School in Leysin, a mountaintop haven above Lausanne and Lake Geneva. Each summer students from all over the world gather to learn French and to enjoy hiking and biking across mountain pastures and slopes. The Swiss mountain pastures are covered with white, pink, and blue wildflowers in summer, and big brown cows with tinkling bells munch and moo their way across these verdant pastures. Each small Swiss village has chalets with brilliant window boxes. Neighbors compete for the most lavish window display. In the following two essays we take a summer pilgrimage to a few of Switzerland's many summer retreats. ❧

Summer Gardens in Switzerland

YOU MIGHT SAY THAT ALL OF SWITZERLAND is a garden. Its cow-filled pastures stretch green and velvety as far as the eye can see. Yellow, pink, blue, and violet flowers bedeck this green sward. As I walked through these pastures, I asked myself, "When did weeds become flowers?" In all directions there were yellow dandelions, purple asters, wild bluebells, native deep purple spikes, and carpets of gray pink mint. As I hiked purposefully up through these pastures, I asked myself, "Why would anyone plant a garden in the midst of one?"

The Swiss are an intensely frugal people. Small carts behind bicycles are filled with newly cut hay for backyard cows. Stacks of precisely cut wood adorn each chalet, ready for winter's gales. In the high pastures, cowherds have covered each cow patty with hay to add to the mulch pile below. This frugality is at the heart of one type of Swiss garden.

A small vegetable garden we found in Kandersteg that fronted an ancient chalet built in 1759 epitomized a beautiful garden with a purpose. A neat square, divided into four parterres with a circular middle, contained a succulent abundance of vegetables. One parterre was iridescent green with Boston lettuce and deep green spinach. Another parterre contained cauliflower and broccoli whose gray-green leaves had droplets of fresh dew. Another parterre was full of yellow-blooming squash and orange-blooming cucumbers. The centerpiece contained cherry tomatoes and red bell peppers. The entire enclosure was flourishing in built-up beds pungent with cow manure. Surrounding this rabbit's delight were small outcroppings of delicately scented herbs: pink- and white-blooming mint of all types; lavender spikes of rosemary; and blue spikes of lavender. Running a hand over the leaves filled the air with a multitude of scents. We settled on a small terrace surrounded by this "Peter Rabbit" garden. A pink and white Swiss damsel served us a cup of tea with fresh lemon mint leaves on the plate. The interior was filled with carved wooden antiques, with a ceramic stove for heating and round lead-rimmed windows. The salad luncheon was juicy with onions, carrots, bell peppers, and lettuce from the abundant garden. Mr. McGregor never had a more perfect garden, or one that would be more appreciated by Flopsy, Mopsy, Cottontail, and Peter.

The Swiss window boxes are like moustaches on a man's face, twinkling and smiling. Some window boxes have red and white geraniums, while others have pink and purple petunias. Still others are packed with pink and purple fuchsias and pink and red begonias. To some the pairing of crimson, violet, scarlet, and orange would seem garish. The cool weather and abundant rainfall assure that these color-ful house trimmings have never-ending blooms. When low gray and white clouds blow in or slanting rainfall with booming thunder drives everyone inside, the bril-liant, colorful window boxes are sparkling and bright.

Swiss landmarks often come with exquisitely designed and planted gardens. Swiss pride was much in evidence at Schloss Spiez, a castle compound dating from 1388 in the small town of Spiez on the Thunersee. The castle with its multiple tile-trimmed spires occupies a fortress position on a rocky outcropping over the lake. Rapunzel might have let down her tresses for the prince from one of those towers. The garden was the entering focal point to the castle with vistas in all directions. One viewpoint was toward neat, green rows of grapes used for making Müller-Thurgau, the white wine that is the specialty of the region. Another vista was toward the lake, whose mother-of-pearl surface was blue, green, or gray, depending on the sky. The garden was the centerpiece with blazes of color drawing the eye for-ward. The entry path was planted thick with standard and very old fuchsias. These flowers, so like dainty dancing ladies, were purple and red, or melon and pink, or rose and lavender. Each breath of wind moved their petals up like skirts so that their tendrils pranced. Six-foot beds surrounded the central greensward. At eye level were blue asters, yellow, orange, and white standard verbenas, footed by blue and red sage, blue ageratum, and masses of pink and red begonias. An orange cat, qui-etly stalking a yellow butterfly, added a humorous note. In the middle of this gar-den was a small fountain, surrounded by white phlox and pink dahlias.

We strolled into the castle's central courtyard and there found the life-sized statue of one of the prior Bubenburg owners. Clad in medieval armor, he proudly stood, protecting his castle and garden. He might have sung to us in Longfellow's words:

> Come, read to me some poem,
> Some simple and heartfelt lay,
> That shall soothe this restless feeling,
> And banish the thoughts of day.
> . . . .
> For, like strains of martial music,
> Their mighty thoughts suggest
> Life's endless toil and endeavor;
> And tonight I long for rest.

Rest he surely had as he stood guard over his dominions.

If you go: There are many small hotels overlooking the Thunersee. The loveliest of these is the Strandhotel Belvédère, with an enchanting garden on the lake. A path leads along the Thunersee and from the hotel into the town. Strandhotel Belvédère Spietz, info@belvédère-spiez.ch. Schloss Spiez is open in all seasons.

The Swiss Alps in July, with a Surprise Visit to Lake Maggiore, Italy

FOR A WORDSMITH IT IS PERPLEXING, even irritating, to suggest that there are times when words fail. We all know those times: intense grief, overwhelming happiness, great beauty. The last is the predicament I touch on here. Place: Faulensee, Switzerland, on the Thunersee. In front of me are the magnificent mountains of the Bernese Oberland and the exquisite shadows of the setting sun over the Thunersee. Enormous green and ochre mountains ruggedly tower over and encircle the gray-green lake. The scene was primitive, even primeval, formed from an upwelling of the crashing of the continental plates against each other eons ago. The lake surface was like mother-of-pearl, with hints of blue, rose, peach, and gray, depending on the mood of the sky. As they say in Switzerland, the weather is changeable, one minute sun, the next cloudy with a hint of rain. But the Swiss also have a saying: "There is no poor weather, only poor gear."

Faulensee was not just a treat for the eyes, but also the ears. The centuries-old village church chimed the hour and the music of the bells echoed over the lake. Cows with tinkling bells grazed on the green and yellow meadows above our hotel, the Seeblick. Gulls were wheeling and mewing. A pair of swans preened their exquisite white feathers in unison. When they held their necks up, they were over three feet tall. Mallard ducks claimed their mates and made a big fuss with their quacking and honking. A paddle-wheel boat blew its horn for customers who might wish to take the lake tour.

Since six A.M. that day, we had been mesmerized by Switzerland. Flying into Zurich into a rising eastern sun, we claimed our rental car and headed south to the Gotthard pass. Italy and the northern Italian lakes were the destination to see the gardens of Isola Bella and Isola Madre in Lake Maggiore. Always have a fallback plan. All the Swiss seemed to be en route to Italy, and the wait to get through the Gotthard Tunnel pass was four hours! My spouse does not wait in lines. At the last exit, we veered right at Wassen toward the Susten Pass and climbed precipitously on dozens of hairpin curves and switchbacks, with bicyclists often leading the way with their muscular legs. The mountains were awash with rivulets cascading down from glaciers. Every crevice in each mountain was gushing water. The water was white and pale green from glacial streams. Porsches and Ferraris whizzed by us on the downhill into Interlaken. We moved at a snail's pace, stopping along the way with amazement to admire the pink, blue, yellow, and white meadow flowers. Faulensee was a perfect destination. The lake water was bracingly cold and so clear that rocks could be seen in every detail. With some hesitation we plunged in, swimming to a lone float. The swimming place was called the "Shadow" because of the high hill with beech trees that shaded it. The locals gathered here every afternoon and seemed amazed that we had found their private swimming hole. The sweet smell of smoke rose from the fire of a gaggle of Swiss youths roasting sausages. Our hotel, the Seeblick, sat directly over the green sea. That night we nestled under huge white down comforters, the window open wide to the sweet sounds of the night. Instead of "Now I lay me down to sleep," I murmured to myself, "All's well that ends well."

Every day is one for outdoor activity in the Bernese Oberland. There is a hiker's paradise up every valley and *wanderwege* for every age and strength. We spent two nights in Kandersteg, a verdant plateau surrounded by glaciers. As we trekked up on ancient hiking paths, we were met coming and going by Swiss families. Precious babies in backpacks were sound asleep. Little girls with Heidi-type plaits were hugging close to proud fathers, while mothers walked in front with young sons. We made no time at all as my mate stopped to speak with each willing group. They seemed amazed that we were from the Vereinigten Staaten, as the German Swiss call the United States. Kandersteg is a small town with a few chalet-type hotels. Our corner room at the Victoria Ritter had two balconies with double French doors and a breathtaking view toward a glacier. Sleeping with open doors, curled up under duvets in mid-August is a real treat for a pair of Southerners. The next day we took the chairlift up to the aqua Oeschinensee and walked through cow-filled meadows to a small hut with a terrace. There we perched and enjoyed French and German conversations. "Where do you live? What do you do? How many children do you have?" I have asked and answered at least ten questions in German, French, and Italian, and so the time eases along, and to my amazement, by listening closely to conversations, I learn new words while appreciating different cultures.

The next day we set out for the famous Grindelwald Valley. Looking south beneath the Wetterhorn, Schreckhorn, Eiger, Mönch, and Jungfrau, the valley is a verdant series of expanding pastures and uplands. We drove up to Scheidegg, parked our car, and walked across fields filled with white, yellow, pink, and blue flowers. Along the way we met an attractive French couple from Grenoble and walked along with them, until a large horsefly bit me and I had to stop and curse the bugs that find me wherever I am. As we meandered to the literally hundreds of steps up to the Grindelwald glacier, we met three lovely ladies from Taormina, Sicily. We talked about the Greek temples of their wonderful island. We then drove up the Gimmelwald Valley to Murren, and we were awestruck by the cascading streams falling freely off glaciers above. Suddenly thunder rumbled, a cold rain began, and we ran for cover returning to our hotel.

The Swiss countryside is perfectly manicured. Something about the culture requires them to love their land, and they plant and tend to it as if it were a garden. Half-timbered medieval style single family chalets of rustic brown wood, stone, and plaster with red-tiled roofs dot the green fields. We in this country are so used to the $$$ sign that trumps all other possible land values. Perhaps because the Swiss have had to carve their country out of precipitous mountains, they accept the magic maxim that land must be developed sparingly and with great care lest its beauty be lost forever. The Swiss themselves are rather old-fashioned. Our dour hotel Mom growled with disapproval every time we asked for more than a glass of ice. Her costume reminded me of my grandmother Nan's outfits combining sandals, ancient skirts, and tops. Her short gray hair was the image of her husband's cut-off "do." Yet her hotel was comfortable, well stocked, with wonderful fish from the Thunersee and immaculate rooms with balconies overhanging the lake.

Saying goodbye to the Thunersee was not easy. At the end of a two-hour drive, we found the lovely French-speaking villages of Vaudoise and Valais. We visited several antique stores in Lausanne, and then we drove to Leysin, which is higher than six thousand feet. Arriving at the Grand Hotel of Madame Bonnelli evoked a moment of remembrance. We had last been there with my mother, Emily Whaley. I could see her comfortably seated with paints in hand, capturing the vista of the valley with the Dents du Midi and the vast sweep of the Tour d'Aï and the Berneuse, watercolors which now grace the walls of our summer home on Lake Summit, North Carolina. We even ordered the steak on a plank that she had so enjoyed. Places, sounds, even smells can evoke the past, and so it was for me.

Despite all this beauty, I still yearned to see the gardens of the Italian lakes. So off we went over the Simplon Pass and down into Italy. We stepped out of our air-conditioned car at Pallanzana into the intense heat of a hot and humid Italian July day. Undaunted we caught a ferryboat, and the cool lake breezes wafted over us on our way to Isola Bella. The Borromini Palace sits grandly atop the island with a seven-level garden as its crown. The garden was ablaze with pink espaliered oleanders, pink climbing roses, white crepe myrtles, and beds of brilliant yellow sun flowers. Tall obelisks were entwined with tangerine trumpet vines. We picked flowers hoping to bring the seed back to Charleston. Finally, overcome with heat, I admitted that coming to Italy in July was a mistake, and I begged to be taken back to Switzerland. We caught the car train from Iselle and were amazingly back at Kandersteg and the Victoria Ritter for the drinking hour. We watched the glacier turn pink with the setting sun. My prayer that night was for a forgiving husband who did not get the last word by saying, "I told you it would be a mistake to leave paradise for an inferno." But then where would we be without such willing husbands?

Vacations do make time slow down. Days are filled with hiking, swimming, reading, people-watching, talking, and eating. There is no particular pattern or regimen, and no tasks to accomplish or problems to solve. It is a time for reflection, for project planning, for dreaming, for anticipation, for inspiration, and for longing for home. Whether one is at Folly Beach or at Faulensee, one still often longs for home. As Sir Walter Scott said,

> Breathes there the man, with soul so dead,
> Who never to himself hath said,
> This is my own, my native land!
> . . . .
> If such there breathe, go, mark him well;
> For him no minstrel raptures swell. . . .

If you go:
Hotel Victoria Ritter, Kandersteg, Switzerland, (Fax 41 (0)33678100),
info@hotel-victoria.ch

Le Grand Chalet Hotel, Leysin, Switzerland, with the marvelous view of the high Alps and glaciers has been run by the Bonelli family for three generations. www.grand-chalet.ch

Seeblick Hotel, Faulensee, Switzerland, info@seeblick.ch (Tel. 41336556080).
Isola Bella on Lake Maggiore is open from March 27 through September 30.
It can be reached by boat from Stresa or Pallanza.

Part 4

French Classical Elegance

French gardens have an elegance that is reminiscent of a beautiful Persian rug or an intricately embroidered lace tablecloth. The inspiration for these patterned gardens stems from André Le Nôtre (1613–1700) and his garden creations for French royalty in the seventeenth century. The gardens of the Île de France, encircling Paris, show the classic designs of Le Nôtre and his nineteenth-century interpreters, Henri (1841–1902) and Achille (1866–1947) Duchene. The gardens of Le Nôtre—Vaux-le-Vicomte, Versailles, and Chantilly—create a feeling of power and wealth. The royal families of France commissioned these grand estates as hunting retreats. The flourishes of parterres with their embroidery are the garden emblem of a Baroque culture. The garden at Vaux-le-Vicomte is beautiful, and the interior of the chateau is filled with fine art. Vaux provides much more than rigid formality. It is richly complex with its intricate plantings of brightly colored annuals surrounded with swirls of boxwood. The Château de Vaux is featured in the following essay, "The Joy of French Gardens." The 170 acres of the garden at Vaux stretch to the horizon as a formal tapestry of boxwood, parterres, promenades, canals, fountains, staircases, statuary, and grottoes. The garden has a single point perspective with an axial layout that can be comprehended in a single glance. This "all at once view" gives a great feeling of satisfaction.

The Château de Vaux was built by Nicolas Fouquet from 1656 to 1660. He was the finance minister of Louis XIV, who jealously confiscated Vaux for himself and sent Fouquet to prison where he died. Luckily Vaux was purchased in 1875 by Alfred Sommier, a wealthy sugar merchant. He restored the garden and château to their former elegance with the assistance of Achille Duchene. Vaux should be the choice if one has time while in Paris for a single great French garden. It pleases with its wonderful formality, the harmony of its noble statuary and clipped yews, and the glamour of the blue, yellow, and white annuals planted in parterres like a giant Aubusson carpet.

Gardens such as Vaux can be found all over France and are visited in the following essays. In the Dordogne Valley there is the Château de Hautefort. In the Loire Valley there is the wonderful, river-spanning Château de Chenonceau with its Diane de Poitiers (1499–1566) garden on one side and its Catherine de Medici (1519–1589) garden in pink and blue on the other. On the Côte d'Azur there is the superb creation of Beatrice Ephrussi de Rothschild, which spans the peninsula of Cap Ferrat with vistas from garden enclaves onto the blue Mediterranean. If one visits the Atlantic coast and La Rochelle, one discovers the same elegant seventeenth-century style at the Château de la Roche-Courbon.

There is much more to French garden style than the formality of seventeenth-century French gardens. France is richly diverse in its geography and climate. If one is looking for pure art, the best garden to visit is that of Claude Monet, a short ride from Paris by car or train. Monet's garden in Giverny was created from 1883 to 1926 and was an inspiration for his paintings. The Clos Normand in front of the house has parallel beds of colorful annuals, perennials, shrubs, and trees. It is an explosion of roses, nasturtiums, sweet peas, delphiniums, fox glove, and irises. Lavenders, whites, and pinks provide a painterly effect. The riot of color produces a sense of joy and delight. One comes through a tunnel to the water garden with its famous Japanese bridge covered with white and lavender wisteria. This is a romantic garden created by Monet for art and entertainment and to provide inspiration. It epitomizes the beauty he found in his surroundings for his art. In the following four essays we visit gardens from the Côte d' Azur, through the Dordogne Valley, along the coasts of Aquitaine, Brittany, and Normandy, through the Loire Valley, and to the gardens surrounding Paris. There we discover the elegance of French gardens. ✿

The Joy of French Gardens

From the Dordogne to the Île de France

FROM THE GIANT LANDSCAPES OF ANDRÉ LE NÔTRE at Versailles and Vaux-le-Vicomte to the small public gardens in every town, French flair with color and design inspires a feeling of joy. A visit to French gardens provides the fun of exploring the widely diverse geography and climate of France.

The gardens at the Château de Versailles and at Vaux-le-Vicomte were originally laid out by André Le Nôtre. The Trianon Palace Hotel in the town of Versailles is an elegant and comfortable hotel for visiting both of these seventeenth-century French gardens. This hotel was the location for the signing of the Treaty of Versailles, which ended World War I. Guest rooms with balconies overlook Louis XIV's hunting preserve. The fields are full of grazing sheep and white cows. The hotel has a delightful breakfast room and terrace that also overlook this peaceful park. The welcoming indoor swimming pool and spa provide the perfect spot for relaxing after a leisurely walk in the park.

From the gate on the Rue de Reine there is an easy ten-minute walk to Le Grand Trianon on the grounds of the Châteaux de Versailles. Le Grand Trianon and its garden, as compared to what one finds at Versailles, are on a human scale. The small U-shaped palace, of pink and gray marble, was created by Louis XIV in 1671 as a retreat from the pomp of the Versailles chateau. The gardens in August were planted in red and lavender dahlias in borders with white delphiniums, white lilies, and blue and purple sage. The red, lavender, and blue color scheme created a joyous purple haze over these colorful and geometric gardens. This garden was the perfect destination for an evening stroll, and during our stays we enjoyed it many times.

The next morning we visited the magnificent gardens of the Château de Versailles. We were lucky to be there on a Sunday in August when all of the fountains were gushing water and all the beds were bursting with bloom. The main axis runs from east to west, beginning at the chateau and descending through a series of terraces and fountains to the cruciform-shaped Grand Canal. The garden has a diverse array of marble statues. Especially appealing were the bronze statues on the rims of the pools that represent the rivers of France. My favorite fountains were the Apollo fountain with its dashing horses and the fountain of Latona and the Lycian peasants whom she had turned into frogs for stirring a pond from which she was led to drink after giving birth. Latona turned them into frogs for their inhospitality, dooming them forever to swim in muddy ponds and rivers. Both fountains splashed lots of water. Louis XIV used the same group of artists to create the chateau and garden at Versailles whom Fouquet had used at Vaux-le-Vicomte. Charles Le Brun is responsible for the statues at Versailles, which form an essential part of the gardens' beauty. Le Nôtre designed the garden and aligned it with the center portal of the chateau.

Another day we visited the garden at Vaux-le-Vicomte, which was finished in 1661 by Le Nôtre for Louis XIV's finance minister, Nicolas Fouquet. This splendid garden and chateau are the epitome of cultivated taste in seventeenth-century France. The garden is a masterpiece of subtle changing levels. On the day of our visit in August, it was exquisitely planted in lavender and white annuals. From a dominant axis on the front steps of the chateau, a broad *tapis vert* (greensward) runs to the horizon, which is marked by a giant statue of Hercules. The interior of Vaux was decorated by Charles Le Brun with marvelous ceiling paintings and elegant gilt furniture. The views over the garden provide a grand and infinite perspective.

Wealthy Parisians discovered the coast of Normandy in the 1890s. Today it is a two-hour drive from the town of Versailles. Upper Normandy, near Dieppe, became an intellectual haven for writers and artists at the end of the nineteenth century. The wooded valleys and rich pasture land created a tradition of gentlemanly provincial gardening. Two superb examples of that tradition are Bois des Moutiers in upper Normandy near Dieppe and Château de Brecy near Bayeux in lower Normandy.

Douce France, in Vieule les Rose, is a perfect hotel for visiting Bois des Moutiers. Douce France has steep, gray slate roofs. It is in a complex of old houses surrounding a courtyard. In early May it was lushly planted with irises, dogwood, and clematis. Nearby, white chalk cliffs beckoned for an evening promenade overlooking the English Channel. We were invited by Guerard Bardot, the owner of Douce France, to visit his nearby chateau. We enjoyed his hospitality, his well-appointed garden, and his frisky Jack Russell terrier, Achilles, who nosed about with playful and determined energy.

We visited Le Bois des Moutiers at Varengeville-sur-Mer the next morning. The house was designed in 1894 by Edwin Lutyens (1869–1944) for Guillaume Mallet (?–1946). The Mallets still own the wonderful Arts and Crafts house whose furniture was created by William Morris. Gertrude Jekyll designed the garden. The garden is very English in style with a series of formal garden rooms extending out from the house. In early May the garden was abloom with white dogwood, white clematis, cream roses, white irises, and white lilies. The entrance to the house was planted in white and blue irises backed with box spheres. A broad path of basket-weave brick was outlined by deep borders planted in white, blue, and purple irises. Two sisters, Claire and Constance Mallet, the granddaughters of Guillaume Mallet, gave gracious tours of the house on our visits. Claire took us on delightful walks toward the sea through dense woods with paths through cathedrals of azaleas and rhododendron, many more than one hundred years old. Her excitement at the swathes of pink, white, and rose blooms was contagious. A feeling of joy mixed with serenity emanates from this perfect house and garden.

Lower Normandy, with its flat beaches bordering the English Channel, was the scene on June 6, 1944, of Operation Overlord, the landing in Normandy. The combined Allied armies under General Eisenhower swept through Caen and Bayeux into bloody confrontation with the Germans. Today the peaceful fields of wheat and the small coastal towns seem surreal against that historical backdrop and the scores of acres of white markers which dot the several Allied and Axis military cemeteries from World War II.

The Château de Brecy in the rural heart of the Seulles River Valley in Normandy is an exquisite, approachable garden with a provincial feeling. The house was built in 1638 and is still in private hands. Its Italian Renaissance style garden climbs four terraces to a grand wrought-iron gate. Each of the terraces is ornamented with carved vases of flowers and fruit and edged by balustrades. One terrace has water parterres with artichoke fountains. Another has matching greenswards with small twin pavilions covered with white clematis. A final terrace is laced with matching borders of boxwood in a *parterre de broderie.* The house and garden were purchased in 1992 by Didier and Barbara Wirth, and both have been immaculately restored. On summer evenings the sun sets in the axis of the portal and illuminates the garden, providing a perfect instant in time.

We enjoyed a private Sunday morning tour of Château Brecy arranged for us by the concierge at the Trianon Palace Hotel at Versailles. When traveling, we are a coalition of the cheerful, always expecting the best is yet to come. Liberally tipping will always facilitate that chance!

The Loire Valley is just two hours south of Paris. Rich alluvial soil and agricultural wealth has existed in the Loire Valley for many centuries. Great houses of the French nobility were built along the Loire and Cher Rivers as early as the fifteenth century. The towns of Tour, Blois, and Amboise make an inviting base for visiting these gardens and their chateaux. Our base for enjoying the gardens of the Loire Valley was Le Vieux Manoir in the heart of old Amboise. We stayed in the Josephine Suite, which looks out on pink summer roses, pink gladiolas, and pink phlox. The breakfast of blueberries and cream in the conservatory looking out on an amply laden fig tree was a special treat.

Who can resist the Château de Chenonceau with its arches and pale stone arcade spanning the waters of the Cher River? Our visit was late one afternoon in August. We had the gardens all to ourselves. We especially loved the Catherine de Medici garden to the right of the entrance. It was planted in blue, white, and yellow annuals with a gurgling central fountain. Diane de Poitiers created the galleried bridge jutting across the Cher River. Her garden graces the left side of the entrance. Eight diagonal parterres were planted in lush green grass and edged in santolina. Narrow beds along the brick walls were filled with colorful annuals. The garden is especially beautiful when viewed from the windows of the chateau. We lingered into the late afternoon, before returning to Le Vieux Manoir for the drinking hour and a delightful walk through the town of Amboise.

If you go:

Trianon Palace Hotel, Versailles (Tel. 33 (0)139845000, Fax 33 (0)130845001), www.TrianonPalace.com

Hotel Douce France, Veules les Roses on the Alabaster Coast of Normandy (Tel. 33235578530), www.hoteldoucefrance.com

Le Vieux Manoir, in Amboise, www.le-vieux-manoir.com or le_vieux_manoir@yahoo.com

The best guide to French gardens is Patrick Taylor's *The Garden Lover's Guide to France.* It provides telephone and fax numbers to each garden, as well as hours for visiting.

Monet's Garden

FINDING GIVERNY FROM ROUTES OTHER THAN PARIS can be a challenge. We had spent the previous night in Chartres to enjoy the exquisite stained glass windows of this 1193 cathedral. We then headed north to Dreux and Evreux, both in the direction of the Seine River. France in early spring is a checkerboard of plowed fields, brilliant green fields of wheat, and yellow fields of rapeseed. Giverny seemed only an hour away, but distances are deceiving in France. We finally arrived at Rolleboise and the Domaine de la Corniche Hotel, reaching Monet's garden at Giverny around noon. Finding Giverny from Paris is an altogether easier experience. If one stays at the Hotel Trianon Palace in Versailles, Giverny is a mere one-hour ride into the countryside of Normandy. Discovering Monet's Garden, by whatever route, is an enticing and delightful experience.

On this early June day the garden was ablaze with color. The garden, a large rectangle, extends beneath Monet's pink farmhouse. The beds of perennials and annuals are about six feet wide and thickly planted in avenues of color. Small pebble paths of two feet separate these blazes of colorful flowers. The garden is planted for peak spring bloom. In Monet's garden the eye is treated to amazing palettes of color. One avenue is composed of blue irises, blue pansies, and pink tulips. Another avenue of color consists of yellow pansies and red and yellow tulips. In Monet's garden color is skillfully brought to eye level with standard peonies and standard roses. Exquisite, heavily scented lilacs of white, lavender, and deep purple form focal points. Overhead color is provided by arbors and by espaliered apple and pear trees. Wisteria was in bloom and cascaded overhead when we visited. The exuberance of color combinations reminded me that Monet's interest in his garden stemmed from his objective of using it for painterly inspiration. Indeed many of Monet's paintings of spring irises have their origin in his garden.

We left the flower garden and walked to Monet's famous water lily garden, where paths meandered along the Epte River, which Monet diverted to create a lake. Bamboo groves give an oriental flavor to the water garden, while rosy red and orange maples enhance the Japanese flavor of the setting. There are benches in shady groves, and we settled into one between two rivulets and listened to birdsong. Monet hired a gardener whose sole task was to maintain his water lilies in perfect condition and in painterly displays. The love of water lilies is evident in many of his paintings. We stopped on the rounded Japanese bridge to touch and smell the wonderful lavender and white wisteria.

We toured Monet's farmhouse and found it to be charmingly furnished and with colorful rooms: a bright yellow dining room with blue porcelain attached to the walls and a blue kitchen with a huge old iron stove. Everywhere there were marvelous nineteenth-century Japanese prints and engravings of courtesans going about their business of dressing, bathing, and talking. The windows beckoned with splendid views of the flower garden in all its spring lushness.

For Monet his garden was a place where sun and shade intermingled with ever-changing colors to extend his artistic palette. A visit to his garden enhanced my own appreciation for color, the very soul of a romantic garden.

If you go: Domain de la Corniche Hotel at Rolleboise, 5 route de la Corniche, Rolleboise—five kilometers from Giverny, on a lovely, high bluff overlooking a crescent bend in the Seine River. La Corniche can be reached at (Tel. 01 30 93 20 00, Fax 01 30 42 27 44). We also visited Monet's garden from the Trianon Palace Hotel in Versailles (Tel. 33 (0)130845000).

France

In Our Own Car

MY GREAT-GRAND AUNT, ELIZABETH "LIZZIE" SINKLER COXE (1843–1918), journeyed to Provence from Paris "in her own car" in 1902 accompanied by her brother Wharton Sinkler of Philadelphia; her son, Eckley Brinton Coxe, of Drifton, Pennsylvania; and her two eighteen-year-old nieces, Emily Sinkler of Belvidere Plantation, South Carolina, and Elizabeth Stevens of Northampton Plantation, South Carolina. Exactly 103 years later, accompanied by my intrepid husband, Fred LeClercq, we set forth in Lizzie's footsteps through Provence. We took the trip in reverse, from Monaco to Paris, while Lizzie journeyed from Paris, ending in Monaco. Lizzie was elated by something that seems so ordinary to us: "No one can imagine until they have tried it, the delight of traveling in Europe in one's own car. From the moment when you see the gigantic box containing the precious thing swung on shore, it is a perpetual pleasure, and most of all interesting to see it dangling in the air like a huge beetle when they put it off at Boulogne." Lizzie described the roads as "broad and smooth with the fields scarlet with poppies." She filled the car with "flowers, baskets of fruit, and even a pair of old brass candlesticks" for dining al fresco (Elizabeth Sinkler Coxe, *Tales from the Grand Tour, 1890–1910,* edited by Anne Sinkler Whaley LeClercq, p. 50–52).

Our beginning seemed inauspicious. We had dropped our Italian car in San Remo, and with bags on shoulders we headed for the train station only to learn that the French trains were on strike and that there were no rail options for getting to Monaco. Undeterred, Fred left the confusion of the train station and found an Italian taxi driver who would take us the twenty-seven kilometers to Monaco. Lorenzo, our cab driver, spoke flawless Italian and French and sped over the *corniche* to our rendezvous at Hertz in Monaco.

We spent the night at the Hotel Welcome in Villefranche. Seated on the 4th floor in a yellow and blue room with double doors, I found my eyes were transfixed by the deep blue Mediterranean. Below small boats of the fishing fleet unloaded their abundant catch of the day. Eager housewives with barking dogs in tow made the day's purchases. A sweet breeze amplified my feeling of serenity as I gazed toward the elegant peninsula of Cap Ferrat, where we stayed on a later trip.

The Grand-Hotel du Cap Ferrat built in 1908 stands on almost seventeen acres of exquisite gardens and indigenous plants at the tip of the famous peninsula bought by King Leopold II of Belgium in the late 1800s. Our room had a vista over the

Alep pine treetops to sea. We dined at Le Cap restaurant with its trompe-l'oeil décor on Carnoroli risotto with langoustines and chicken confit with fois gras and black truffles. We breakfasted and swam in the lower pool reached by an all-glass funicular during a trip that offered views of the sea and the original semitropical vegetation. We took long walks around the peninsula's lovely private homes and gardens and to its lighthouse and enjoyed the hotel's fine spa and service. Most important of all, the hotel is in close proximity to the Rothschild estate and other lovely gardens in the area. As our dear friend Tennessee law professor Durward Jones might have said, "What's *not* to like about this place?"

There is a saying that it is impossible to have a bad meal in France. Beginning with breakfast, I was delighted to find a repast so delicate and so delicious that I could eat breakfast all day. I enjoyed shirred eggs, sausages, delicate cheeses, ham, sweet rolls, and most important, hot Earl Grey tea. Our destination for the morning was the Rothschild garden, sitting elegantly on the brow of St.-Jean-Cap-Ferrat.

My great-grand aunt, Lizzie, who loved violets and bunches of lilies and had planted her beautiful garden at Windy Hill in Drifton, Pennsylvania, with rows of blue hydrangeas, would surely have visited this garden of Baroness Rothschild's. Oh, how I would have loved to have had Lizzie with me at the Rothschild garden, the perfect creation of another Belle Epoque lady, Beatrice Ephrussi de Rothschild.

There were actually nine gardens, each representing a different culture or nationality. The unifying theme that bound the entirety together was the superb paths and the enchanting use of water, which twinkled and splashed everywhere in each of the gardens. The other unifying factor was the vista of the blue-green Mediterranean, framed by the masses of pines, olive trees, and venerable cypresses.

The exquisite pink villa is fronted by a symmetrical French garden. From the steps of the villa, we could see a musical fountain, green velvet squares of grass, and a watercourse planted richly in yellow and orange calendulas. The focal point in the distance is a sumptuous waterfall that cascades down from the Temple of Love, a circular Doric temple where Venus reigns. Other gardens spread in all directions: a Japanese garden with a bamboo watercourse, a Spanish garden richly planted in oranges and filled with the sound of water, an architectural garden containing the remains of delicate stone carvings and artifacts. I longed for the key to the garden gate so that I might sit on an iron bench and watch the sea turn violet as the pink sun descends into the Mediterranean. We toured the villa, a veritable treasure house of porcelains, paintings by Fragonard, and delicate satins and silks of the Belle Epoque. Each lovely room looked out onto the garden, a delicate and verdant scene. It is too bad when a perfect day must end. As I look back, I think we might have stayed there for a week or a year. Cap Ferrat and Beaulieu-Sur-Mer have a perfect setting—why leave the Garden of Eden? But we picked up and followed in Lizzie's footsteps to Aix. Fred did a masterful job of driving over the Alpilles, verdant with pine trees, olive orchards, and vineyards, while the huge and towering Alps loomed in the distance.

We enjoyed the Boulevard Mirabeau in Aix, with the statue of King René of Anjou (1409–1480), who brought wine culture to Provence. We mingled with the amazingly young student population that made the town seem like King Street when the College of Charleston is in session. Instead of staying, we decided to spend the night in Arles and immerse ourselves in Roman ruins. Lizzie had especially loved Arles.

Arles is small, the size of an old Roman town, with ancient ochre houses built on the visible remains of the Romans' structures. We stayed at the D'Arlatan, a superb and ancient home of the dukes of Arles. Breakfast was in the salon, looking out onto a quiet courtyard with a small fountain in which four live turtles were swimming and sunning. We followed Lizzie's directions and went to "the street of the Dead with its many fine old Roman sarcophagi and the beautiful old Amphitheatre."

We left Arles, intending to spend the night at the Hotel d'Europe in Avignon, where Lizzie had actually spent the night in the same room that Napoleon had occupied on his return from Elba. The imperious French attendant showed us the room that opened onto a sunlit courtyard, which was redolent with the scent of purple lilacs and wisteria. Alas, when the receptionist informed us that the room was 750 Euros for one night, we thanked him graciously and departed in haste.

We sped over the autoroute from Avignon, through Orange, and on to Valence, amazed by the new green fields alternating with bright yellow fields of rapeseed. Finally we entered the mountains of the Madeleine, where lovely white Charolais cows dined and dallied. We covered over 350 miles in four hours, finding our way to Vichy, where Lizzie had spent two nights. Vichy was the epitome of the Belle Epoque watering spot, with its hot baths, casino, and grand towering hotels. How times had changed. Lizzie described it as filled with "fashionable crowds visiting the springs and the gay Casino and Parisian shops and the beautiful park where all day long people sat and read and embroidered under the lindens and plane trees while pretty string bands played."

The bandstands are still there, and the elaborately decorated ten-story hotels adorned with cherubs, garlands of roses, and grand nudes stand as vestiges of a grand spa of another era. But the elegant throngs are long gone. We joined the afternoon promenade in the verdant green park along the Allier River. The park extends for miles on both sides of the river, with a golf course, tennis courts, and race track on the far side. There were enormous groves of huge old shade trees: marron in bloom, sycamores with their new balls, huge ilex, and red-leafed beech. Vichy is a shadow of its former self, yet still a charming, small, and elegant place to visit. We rented bicycles and explored Vichy on the town's splendid bicycle paths.

We left Vichy with the intention of visiting both the Cathedral of St. Etienne in Bourges and the Cathedral of Notre Dame in Chartres. Lizzie had visited both. She commented especially on the Black Madonna, which she mistakenly placed in St. Etienne. Both cathedrals date from the twelfth century and are built in the splendid Gothic style. In St. Etienne we were overcome with the old damp, musty smell of long-gone generations but found a sparkling silver Madonna. The trip from Bourges to Chartres was over old roads in the twinkling light of dusk. Loamy brown fields gave away to rich deep-green fields of wheat and brilliant yellow fields of rapeseed. Finally the spires of Chartres Cathedral appeared in the falling light, rising huge and massive from the flat surrounding fields. We entered the ancient medieval cathedral and "read" each amazing carved scene from the life of Christ. There we discovered the Black Madonna, darkened through the ages as it was carved out of pear wood.

And then one of those mishaps occurred that reminded me that Lizzie had had the misfortune of having her young husband, Charles Brinton Coxe, die on their first trip to Egypt when he was only thirty years old. I could only imagine the agony and difficulty she must have had at getting his body home to Philadelphia. I looked around me as I left the cathedral, and Fred had disappeared. I assumed he had gone into a nearby shop. But when I entered and asked if anyone had seen the man with the bow tie, they said no such person had been there. So I walked back to the hotel, and still no Fred. I headed back to the cathedral, searched inside, and, finding no one, imagined that he had been spirited away by some angry gargoyle. To my utter relief there he was in our room when I returned to the Grand Monarch Hotel, peacefully reading a *Herald Tribune*.

I could only wonder at the strength and perseverance of Lizzie Coxe. We had undertaken in one week a trip that took her six weeks in an open-air car traveling at twenty-five miles an hour on dirt roads. We, however, had sped over superior French highways in a new Renault going more than eighty miles per hour. The journey had carried us to lovely, unfamiliar parts of France such as Vichy and Bourges. Thanks to my great-grand aunt, Lizzie, it is a journey that I will relive many times through memory.

If you go:
Grand-Hotel du Cap Ferrat, www.grand-hotel-cap-ferrat.com

Hotel Welcome, Villefranche (Tel. 0493762762); www.welcomehotel.com

Hotel Arlatan, Arles, hotel-arlatan@wanadoo.fr (Tel. 33490935666)

Hotel Grand Monarque, Chartres, info@bw-grand-monarque.com (Tel. 0237181515)

Be sure to take Patrick Taylor's *The Garden Lover's Guide to France.*

Chateau of Chenonceau in the Loire Valley, France

The house and garden at Bois des Moutiers in Normandy, France

Left: The author in the garden at Giverny, Vernon, France

The Japanese bridge in Monet's water garden, at Giverny, Vernon, France

Fred LeClercq in the garden of
Chateau Brecy near Caen, France

Below: The chateau and garden of
Vaux le Vicomte near Paris, France

The Atlantic Coast of France

Off the Beaten Track

I KNOW THE SOUR SIDE OF THE FRENCH, the Parisian waiters who denigrate my Charleston-accented French! How delightful then to discover that off the beaten track there are happy, smiling, accepting French. The virtues of French culture were on display during a recent June visit to the Atlantic coastal region. I delighted in the family gatherings: grandparents, grown children, and babies enjoying their beautiful land. I thrilled at a verdant, agricultural countryside of vineyards, wheat fields edged in poppies, and pastures full of white, grazing cows. I melted at the gastronomy of fresh raspberries, delicate omelets, sautéed mushrooms, sole meuniere, and lush desserts. I thrilled at the lilting language that floats and sings. I discovered that I could still sing "Sur le Pont" and mime "Monsieur le Corbet" from my early years at Charleston Day School and Ashley Hall.

One of the high points of our visit was Versailles and Hotel Le Grand Trianon. Set in the sumptuous gardens Le Nôtre built for the Sun King, Louis XIV, Le Grand Trianon is a vibrant jewel. A Sunday afternoon stroll in the Versailles gardens, with its vast array of gushing fountains is a marvelous experience. We then ventured to the Château de Chantilly to see the stunning Condé art collection assembled by Duke Aumale. The garden by André Le Nôtre has majestic formal water gardens reflecting the venerable chateau. There was also a 600-foot-long stable that could house 240 horses. The former owner who built the stable is said to have believed in reincarnation. He must have expected not only to come back as a horse, but as a horse at Chantilly. Our Hotel Le Grand Trianon at Versailles was an amazingly convenient location for visiting Paris, combining our love for the Paris area while enjoying the country life of chateaux and their objets d'art and gardens.

We left Paris for Normandy, the D-Day beaches, and Port en Bassin. We stayed at the Hotel Mercure, whose golf course overlooks the Omaha Beach landing area. That night I walked the golf course, built on these old killing fields, and marveled that our troops made it up the steep hillsides of Omaha Beach. We stopped at the nearby garden of Domain du Plantbessin. An always welcoming Collette and Hubert Sainte-Beuve were excited for us to see their extraordinary garden adjacent to their nursery. With twelve garden "rooms," they had the perfect space to show off clematis, wisteria, alliums, lilacs, and water lilies. Collette had black earth under every fingernail and was gritty. Hubert described her: "like everyone from

Brittany, an artichoke, a bit prickly." He was tall and fashionable with a silk scarf. When I asked her if he helped out, she smiled and said, "Yes, he will feed the fish."

We were greatly impressed with Château de Balleroy, also in Normandy, built by the French architect François Mansart (1598–1666), and later purchased by Malcolm Forbes of the Forbes publishing empire. Forbes, a pilot, had been in the World War II Overlord assault. He came back in the 1970s to purchase this chateau. We toured the chateau and garden, enjoying a house that is still lived in by the Forbes family on vacations. The house has the intimate feel of personal collections including balloon memorabilia, highly polished silver on tables, paintings by Albert Balleroy, letters and photographs from Lyndon Johnson, and pictures with Nancy and Ronald Reagan. Yellow climbing roses cling to the walls of the garden.

We left Normandy for the coast of Brittany and Dinard in the midst of a four-day French holiday. We found the last hotel room, truly wonderful, in Dinard at Grand Hotel Barriere. I could have stayed there for the month. We bicycled along the Route de la Mer. I swam in the hotel's wonderful open-air swimming pool. The vista of St. Malo over the bay was blue and full of sailboats. Children were building sand castles while adults sunbathed.

Sometimes chance intervenes in our lives, and we take an unexpected yet productive direction. So it was with our stay at Les Brises Hotel, on the old port of La Rochelle, its harbor dotted with sailboats and kayaks. One morning we ventured to nearby Lucon to see the town garden. We were admiring the vast Gothic cathedral when Father Pierre Chatry offered to give us a tour. When I asked the way to the local town garden, he responded that we should visit the garden of his friend William Christie. A visit was arranged. We wended our way through green fields of wheat to the tiny town of Thiere. We reveled in Christie's old farmhouse and his welcoming cats, and we talked with his chief gardener, David. Christie's French-style garden is composed of hornbeam hedges surrounding topiary of boxwood, with beds full of double white roses. Stone monuments and spouting water serve as focal points. Rosa, one of the cats, meowed and curled around my legs, leaping in the air occasionally to catch a bug or chase a lizard. Purple and white perennials, pink peonies, and purple irises were abuzz with bees. By chance, we had happened on this engaging morning and the welcoming hospitality of a gracious priest.

At Carcassonne in southwestern France, we stayed at the Orient Express Hôtel de la Cité, perched within its ancient medieval walls. An aunt had warned that I would find Carcassonne a tourist emporium. Staying within the quiet walls of Hôtel de la Cité largely insulated us from tourists. Above the gardens there were vistas to the blue hillsides in the distance. The yellow walls with their pepper-pot towers provided the perfect place for an afternoon walk. I swam each evening in a delightful swimming pool surrounded by cypress and backed by the cathedral. Best yet for a librarian and lover of books, the hotel bar was La Bibliothèque Bar! Carcassonne was our base for touring nearby towns. The region had once been the home of the Cathars, a Christian sect that believed that baptism was the only essential sacrament. The town of Albi on the Tarn River became their capital. It was also the home of Toulouse-Lautrec, and the Palais de la Berbie houses the Toulouse-Lautrec Museum. Below the ramparts, overlooking the Tarn River, is a perfect French garden in the seventeenth-century style. Filled with colorful annuals, the clipped and rounded sheaflike patterns resembled embroidery.

Our Paris to Nice adventure had all too soon come to an end. The small towns and gardens of France, off the beaten track, had a vibrancy, beauty, and immediacy that made my spirits soar. I will be back.

If you go:
reservations@hoteldelacite.com and www.hoteldelacite.com

www.trianonpalace.com

www.hotelbrises-la-rochelle.federal-hotel.com

www.dinardgrandhotel.com

info@hotel-omaha-beach.com

Be sure to read *Omaha Beach: V Corps' Battle for the Beachhead,* by Tim Kilvert-Jones.

Part 5

A Plantsman's Paradise

ENGLAND, WALES, SCOTLAND, AND IRELAND

The British Isles are redolent with bloom from early spring to late autumn. In the following essays we visit gardens as far north as Dunrobin in Scotland and as far south as Muckross in Killarney, on the most westerly tip of Ireland. When I think of gardens in the British Isles, I think of color. Gertrude Jekyll (1843–1932) in her book *Colour Schemes for the Flower Garden* established the parameters for the successful use of color in flower gardens. Her garden at Munstead Wood was the epitome of nineteenth- and twentieth-century garden plantsmanship. Jekyll's theory of color was to establish drifts of harmonious color through plants of related hue. She favored an impressionistic effect so that colors blend and fuse. Believing in the fine art of gardening, she envisioned a garden as a treasure of well-set jewels. In the perfect Jekyll garden there would be drifts of blue and mauve flowers such as the blue geranium jolly bee or Johnson's blue, backed by the lavender of eryngium or even taller blue delphiniums, campanula, agapanthus, or scabiosa. Next to this blue and mauve cluster, she would plant a white drift of clematis, vinca, phlox, cleome, and daisies. A Jekyll garden would use white to soften and combine primary colors or to enliven greens and give sparkle to a garden. Jekyll advised that, when planting blue, set it off with yellow such as achillea or macrocephalia, as she maintained that yellow makes blue less melancholy and helps to define it. A Jekyll garden will have a restful mood through the use of harmonizing colors. Barrington Court, featured below, has an enclosed, walled garden with a white color scheme designed by Jekyll. On a May visit it displayed elegance and style that was dazzling.

The following essays on gardens in the British Isles highlight the joy of visiting several gardens created according to the color theory of Gertrude Jekyll.

Scotland abounds in stylish, flower-filled gardens. Some of my favorites include Culzean, near Turnberry, warmed by the North Atlantic drift with a walled garden designed by Robert Adam in 1786; Threave, in Galloway, with more than 175 acres, including a walled garden whose mixed fall border is of pink astilbes, white daisies, white astilbes, and white phlox; Torosay Castle and Garden on the Isle of Mull, designed by David Bryce, with terraces and statues reminiscent of an Italian garden; Brodick Castle and Garden on the Isle of Aran, with a plant collection spanning China and other spots in Asia, South America, and New Zealand; Drummond

Castle Gardens near Perth, which dates from the 1630s and sings with the French single-point perspective design; Crathes Castle and Garden dating from 1543, which has eight color-themed "garden rooms" planted after Gertrude Jekyll in blue, gold, and white backed by old Portugal laurels; Kinross House, just north of Edinburgh and designed by William Bruce in 1675 as his own home and garden, and overlooking Loch Leven, where Mary, Queen of Scots, was imprisoned; Kellie Castle in Fife, which was the home of Robert Lorimer in the 1870s and whose Dorothy Perkins roses curve around pergolas and roundels. And in southwestern Ireland, away from Scotland, we explore lush green gardens, including Bantry House and Garden, Dunloe Castle and Gardens, Glin Castle, and Muckross Castle and Garden.

In each of these gardens, ask yourself the following questions: How have flowers been melded together to create a painterly effect? How have flowers been chosen by size to create a three-dimensional impact? How have hedges been used to set off borders filled with flowers? What color themes are used and in which seasons?

England is also known for its elaborate formal and informal water gardens. We consider water gardens that are rich with landscape water designs, such as Capability Brown's temple-filled water paradise at Stourhead. Equally impressive are more recent water designs such as that of Harold Peto at Buscot Park, which combines the formal use of fountains, pools, cascades, and bridges with an informal artificial lake with a traditional temple on the far shore. Water, whether it is in motion through water staircases or cascades or is reflective, as in pools or lakes, is a powerful garden tool. British countryside gardens are a showcase for its effective use. ∿

Chewton Glen and
Exbury Garden, England

CHEWTON GLEN IN HAMPSHIRE, ENGLAND, is recommended by the Relais and Château Hotel group. It is much more than an elegant place to stay; it is a great destination for visiting England in May to relish the sweet smells of lilacs and wisteria and to witness the colorful abundance of rhododendron and wild azaleas. Our adventure began at Exbury Gardens, the two hundred-acre estate that Lionel de Rothschild acquired on the Beaulieu River in 1919. Rothschild planted trees such as copper beeches, cedars, and holm oaks that form a green backdrop for a diverse woodland planting of more than two thousand camellias and thousands of crimson, red, and yellow rhododendron. Chief gardener John Anderson, a delightful Irishman, guided us through the charms of this exuberant garden.

Anderson toured us through the park, whose central feature is three reflecting pools connected by stair-step waterfalls. He advised that maintaining a garden of this size was all about balancing: balancing shade and light; balancing moisture and drought; pruning and letting plants grow. He noted that this part of England has only twenty inches of rain a year, making a watering system essential. The grass paths were easy on the feet and led to a vista of sailboats on the Beaulieu River. Anderson, with his keen Irish wit, told us that the secret to the Rothschild's longevity was fresh air, chocolate, wine, and a dictionary that excluded the word *cholesterol!* He enjoyed the challenge of working for Rothschild, a man who always had a new vision. Their current project is to create more fall color through the planting of tupelo trees and purple Japanese maples.

We found our hotel, Chewton Glen, which is located in New Milton, just off the English Channel. The hotel sits on sixty acres of gardens. We swam in the inviting outdoor swimming pool. On taking the thirty-minute walk down to the coast, we found the waves pummeling the shore. The hydrotherapy baths were enjoyable, and each morning there was the requisite workout in a perfectly equipped gym. We dined at the hotel's acclaimed Marryat Restaurant and breakfasted on smoked salmon and mouth-watering croissants laced with lemon curd. We were served attentively by young waiters from France, Poland, Hungary, Spain, and Germany as well as England.

A walk around the grounds with the head gardener, Darren Venerable, gave me new insight into the problems of being associated with the European Union. Each year places open to the public must hire a tree surveyor who inspects every tree, ordering those cut down that might pose any hazard. At Chewton Glen many old beeches had been demolished as a result of the inspector's orders. Another regulation requires the daily keeping of the amount of water used on the place. Darren was proud of his well-kept blue and white herbaceous borders that were framed by a lavender and white wisteria pergola. Darren's kitchen garden contained all the herbs used at the bar and also in the kitchen. He proudly showed me the beds of Butlers' sorrel for soups and spearmint for the bar.

We were not surprised to learn that Chewton Glen has been awarded many accolades including the Walpole award for British Luxury Service as well as the Gallivanter's Guide Award for being one of the several best small hotels under one hundred rooms in the world. Our third-floor suite had a bucolic vista of the meadow and stream and the forests beyond. My greatest pleasure was walking the grounds and discovering the beauty of the English countryside in May. We dawdled our way along a riverside path next to a meadow below the hotel and came upon countless azaleas, rhododendron, and wildflowers in full bloom. As we meandered the carefully manicured fairways and greens of the hotel's nine-hole, three-par golf course, we recalled Ben Hogan's admonition, "Want to improve your putting game? Chip close to the pin!"

If you go:
Exbury Gardens, www.exbury.co.uk, below Southampton near Beaulieu

Chewton Glen, www.chewtonglen.com, New Milton, Hampshire, England

Le Manoir aux Quat'Saisons, Buscot Park, and Waddesdon Manor, England

ELEGANCE IS A TERM THAT HAS MULTIPLE and sometimes diverse definitions. It generally implies a quality of being refined, stylish, or, perhaps, in the fashion of the day. But elegance can also imply a sublime level of comfort and an inviting freshness. Such a comparison might be made between Waddesdon Manor, the 1877 chateau of Ferdinand de Rothschild (1839–1898), and Le Manoir aux Quat'Saisons, a superb Orient Express hotel and garden.

Ferdinand de Rothschild was an omnivorous collector of fine arts. He had Waddesdon, his elegant, late-empire-style chateau, constructed to contain his collections and to immerse himself in the company of the English royalty and gentry whom he lavishly entertained. He attracted the well-to-do of Western Europe to his palace to pay homage to his wealth and aesthetic sensibility and perhaps to cast envious eyes on his Reynolds and Gainsborough portraits, his Meissen and Sevres porcelain, his lacquered English and French furniture, his porcelain sculpture, his elegant marble statues, his Savonnerie carpets, and his centuries-old Continental tapestries.

Waddesdon Manor is the second most-visited of Britain's outstanding National Trust properties. On a bank holiday Monday in May, the place was teaming with ordinary folk enjoying a day on a larger-than-life, Biltmore-scale estate. Waddesdon resonated with style from its steep, blue-slate-roofed, Chambord-styled corner towers to the unique collections adorning its interior. Above every mantle there was a superb cut-glass mirror, centered with magnificent French clocks, heavy with the voluptuous figures of Greek and Roman goddesses attended by cherubs and pursued by mortals or gods as handsome as Apollo and as sure-footed as Mercury. The clocks, as always in National Trust properties, ticked the correct time in unison. Matching pairs of blue Sevres or hand-painted Meissen urns adorned the mantles and were dispersed as focal points on various tables. The house and garden are classic French. The walls and furnishings in many of the rooms were acquired as a result of Haussman's widening of the boulevards of Paris in the mid-1800s. Rothschild had the wherewithal to buy unique, priceless antiquities dispersed in the excesses of the French Revolution. The manor house was designed by Gabriel-Hippolyte Destailleur (1822–1893) and was finished in 1880. The garden was laid out by Elie Laine and contains a wealth of exquisite Italian statues. The ensemble is comparable to the Biltmore Estate in Asheville, with its formal gardens and French architectural style.

Waddesdon and Biltmore are elegant and refined, but are they comfortable? Our world of elegance is defined by an inordinately higher level of creature comforts. Le Manoir aux Quat'Saisons represents the apotheosis of the greatest creature comforts available through twenty-first-century technology combined with the refined taste and good judgment without which stylish, elegant, comfortable living is impossible. Only a thirty-minute drive from the Rothschild estate, just below Oxford near Great Milton, Le Manoir aux Quat'Saisons is an elegant Relais and Château manor house with every creature comfort. Our suite, "Blanc en Blanc," with its wrought-iron entry gate, led to a stone path embedded with ancient millstones. The path's borders had a mass of yellow-centered, white daisies that lay at the feet of perfectly clipped and rounded yews. The entire entrance to our suite was enclosed by an old stone wall so that its natural effect was that of a private garden within a larger garden. The sense of privacy was enhanced by neatly trimmed borders of different trees, which extended above our small garden's four-foot-high walls.

There was much more outside our suite. The garden with its Japanese Tea Room House and three lakes was replete with ducks and the charm of the sky's reflections. There were blue and white lupines and delphiniums growing in the borders, and while pink peonies edged the huge vegetable garden. The vegetable garden is the picking plot of Chef Raymond Blanc, the noted French culinary king of Le Manoir. Our greatest delight was in the chef's dinner. I had sea bass with a white sauce of herbs from the garden. Fred had a filet of beef with a dark, rich wine sauce, plentifully served with mushrooms. Raymond Blanc had grown up in France in the village of Besancon. There his father had drawn maps for him on where to find the choicest mushrooms. As he summarized in his book *A Taste of My Life,* of all the mushrooms in the world, petit gris is the most perfumed, which is fortunate because he had to hunt them by smell as well as by sight. To re-create his childhood memories, Chef Blanc began a five-year project in making a mushroom valley at Le Manoir. A ravine was chosen and edged with silver birch and oak. A spore incubator was built to cultivate the mushroom spores. When the spores are ready, they are drilled into the logs. Chef Blanc hopes to grow more than twelve different types of mushrooms for the table, including shiitake, king stropharia, parasol, maitake, and cauliflower fungus to provide fresh mushrooms over the course of the year. Le Manoir has elegance as well as soul. This is a destination where great cuisine and warm hospitality invite the weary traveler to relax and enjoy.

The most stunning garden we enjoyed close to Le Manoir was Buscot Park. It is the manorial home of Lord and Lady Faringdon and comprises several separate and distinct gardens: (1) a formal, walled garden with herbaceous borders that includes a purple wisteria-covered pergola in full bloom and enclosed on its sides by an espaliered red-bud covered with small, pink flowers; (2) the famous water garden designed by Harold Peto (1854–1933), descending a gentle incline with flowing cascades to a large lake replete with garden and water statuary and central and cross-axis focal-point vistas; and (3) grass paths in a landscape garden harmoniously extending into the woodlands from the axes of the formal, walled garden and the water garden.

The formal garden is enclosed by an old red-brick wall, about fifteen feet in height. Enormous clumps of peonies filled with scores of buds were showing pink and white color and about to burst into bloom. An espaliered fig tree heavy with fruit covered one large section of the brick wall. The entry to the walled garden took us by a glass house where the head gardener, Peter Auger, was busy working in the greenhouse. He proved a fountain of information about Harold Peto's work at Buscot Park in the creation of the water garden. Between the house and an ornamental lake, Peto's stepped water garden makes its stately progress down a gentle wooded incline. Across the lake a domed, pillared temple provides a marvelous focal point.

England in May has roses coming into bloom while laburnums, rhododendron, wild azaleas, clematis, and lavender and white wisteria are a blaze of fragrant blossoms. Each of our destinations provides a different perspective on English gardens in May. The formal Victorian gardens of Waddesdon Manor have colorful annual bedding schemes in place, while the grounds are alive with classical Italian statues. Le Manoir is the perfect cottage garden with lavender irises and peonies marking every path, and Buscot Park has a magnificent walled garden filled with huge purple allium borders along its grassy paths. A May visit to each is an adventure whose memory will linger.

If you go:

Le Manoir aux Quat'Saisons, Church Rd., Great Milton, Oxford, www.blanc.co.uk. Waddesdon Manor, near Aylesbury, Buckinghamshire, www.wadesdon.org.uk.

Buscot Park in Oxfordshhire, 3 miles NW of Faringdon on A417, open March to September.

Stourhead and the Danesfield House Hotel, England

LONDON IS SURROUNDED BY EXQUISITE ESTATES where the countryside has been land-scaped to include towering trees, rhododendron in profusion, and lakes that mirror the sky and temples. We were lucky to find the best of these, Stourhead, for a walk in an ideal setting during May.

From the Italian Renaissance, Western preferences in gardens have generally leaned to the formal, carefully designed and balanced parterres radiating from the central axis of the manor house or castle. Even the grandest British herbaceous borders, at Levens Hall and Culzean, for example, are based on mathematical and geometric models of balance, which they share in common with the gardens of the Italian Renaissance. The primary difference is that the great British formal gardens rely on a rash of color from annuals and perennials to evoke the sense of satisfaction and pleasure achieved in the Italian Renaissance with statuary, fountains, pools and manicured shrubs such as boxwood or yew.

The British landscape garden or park offers a competing model to the Italian Renaissance formal garden with different aesthetic postulates and principles. Stourhead is an iconic example of the British landscape garden. The landscape garden is a gently idealized version of nature which incorporates the fields, hills, forests and streams of the wider countryside. The model of the landscape garden was landscape painting, and the task of the gardener was to compose picturesque garden views with all of the freedom of the landscape painter.

The forty-acre landscape park at Stourhead was begun in 1741 by the banker Henry Hoar II in (1705–1785). Hoar's masterstroke was the dam across the western end of the valley, which turned a series of fishponds into a single sheet of water. He conceived a counterclockwise circuit walk around the new lake, thus linking garden buildings and picturesque views in a carefully contrived sequence. Stourhead had been occupied since William the Conqueror invaded England in 1066, and Henry Hoar tore down the nearby castle that had belonged to the Stourton family to make way for his manor house. The house is an elegant Palladian masterpiece filled with collections of paintings and statues from Italy.

We meandered through the park, which was ablaze with crimson, pink, and yellow hybrid rhododendron. We walked across the Palladian bridge and marveled at the domed Pantheon (1753) on the far shore of the lake. The grass-covered bridge had a quacking family of ducks. We walked through the Temple of Flora built above the Church of St. Peter. But our greatest delight was Henry Flitcroft's

(1697–1769) Temple of Apollo (1765) derived from a Roman original at Baalbec in Syria. Lovely grass walks alternated with gravel, leading us to discover the beauty of images and reflections off the lake, as well as a dozen or more exquisitely framed views. How could we complain? What was not to like about this magnificent estate? As Horace Walpole said in 1762 of the Pantheon, "Few buildings exceed the magnificence, taste, and beauty of this temple."

Our destination for the evening was London by the M3, M25, and finally the ninth exit at Maidenhead to Marlowe and the Danesfield House Hotel. Sitting in the Chiltern Hills overlooking the Thames, this magnificent private home, now a hotel, sits on sixty-five acres of glorious gardens. Our room, the Victoria, overlooked a seventeenth-century knot garden of boxwood enclosed by yew topiary. The Thames that Sunday was full of canoes and yachts and, across from us, on the opposite shore, people walking and dogs swimming. I asked an attendant about going down for a swim. He seemed appalled and said that it was strictly prohibited to swim in the weirs. I assured him that I would keep my swimming to the Danesfield's Spa with its lovely enclosed indoor swimming pool that was "ozone" filtered. We relaxed in the sun and marveled that the English countryside was so unspoiled.

If you go: Stourhead in located in Wiltshire, and is 3 miles NW of Mere by the A303 and B3092. Danesfield House Hotel is located in Marlow, www.danesfieldhouse.co.uk.

Gravetye Manor and
William Robinson, England

THE "WILD" MEADOW THAT FRONTS GRAVETYE MANOR was at the heart of William Robinson's vision of a natural yet cultured landscape. I was meandering down a grass-mown trail to the lake edge. A carpet of iridescent bluebells spread under the blooming apple trees, all redolent with the sweet aroma of May. Behind me was the imposing silhouette of Gravetye Manor, pale yellow Sussex sandstone under a bright blue sky. As I wandered along the path, I noticed a startling yellow sign with flashing bolts of lightning, warning one not to touch the nearby electric fence erected to prevent the large herds of deer from entering the garden. But white-tailed deer are great jumpers and can and do jump fences. "Can anything keep deer out of the garden?," I asked our young garden guide. Thinking back to the deer's primordial fear, now instinctual, as the prey of the greater beasts, my guide quickly responded, "Lion manure, madam."

Dave Garman, a handsome twenty-one-year-old Gravetye gardener who lives on the estate in a tiny cottage just above the oval-shaped walled garden, toured us through the lush spring garden. With glee I caressed first the rosemary and then thyme, and finally I effortlessly grabbed a stinging nettle. With a gasp I cried, "ouch!" Dave diagnosed the problem immediately, grabbed a "doc" leaf and urged me to rub it on my stinging and sore fingers.

There is another challenge for the eager gardener—we are beset with varmints, weeds, and blights, all of which are a true challenge for the gardener who follows in the footsteps of William Robinson (1838–1935). My guide, Dave, recited his many weed challenges. There was bind weed with its deep root and a stinging sap, which would grow among the roses, geraniums, and blue forget-me-nots. The long border was lush with pink peonies, deep purple alliums, and bright pink bleeding heart. But intermixed was that cursed bind weed for which the only remedy was RoundUp. Not far away was Japanese nut weed enjoying the natural habitat of the "Little Garden," which was lush with lavender and white irises and pink and lavender columbines. This had to be extracted laboriously by hand.

Dave is one of only four gardeners managing the immense estate of Gravetye. In Robinson's day there had been nineteen! The ancient manor house, built in 1598, has mullioned windows that bring the formal gardens and lush meadows into the interior. Just under my window was the formal garden with its four green squares, each edged with a flagstone walk. To my right, through a curtain of pink clematis, was the rhododendron and wild azalea garden in bloom with a mix of pink and yellow plants. Just behind that brilliant hillside were the Corsican pines brought back by Robinson from one of his plant-gathering trips abroad. For Dave Garman the extraordinary growth of a "sucker" limb on one of those pines had become another major challenge: how to prune a giant and imposing century-old pine? The sad answer in this case was an unexpected snowstorm!

Gravetye Manor itself was abuzz with the sounds of happy travelers enjoying the ambience of Robinson's wonderful home site. William Robinson was a feisty Irishman with a sharp wit. A man of prodigious personal energy, he rebelled against the accepted order of the Victorian gardener and the huge formal gardens of the French Renaissance. Robinson admonished us that there is no need to mow the long and pleasant grass. He railed at "extensive mowing" of immense lawns or pastures. A small path of access is not contrary to his philosophy of gardening.

Robinson's Gravetye is surrounded by several small formal gardens planted mainly in perennials in the immediate vicinage of the manor. But the extensive hills and meadows of his estate do not need to be mowed. Far better that they should be cultivated with perennial native and exotic wildflowers that provide a diversity of changing color from late winter to late autumn. Narrow access paths beaten down by frequent use or occasional mowing are proper means of facilitating access to the wild gardens of the hillsides, meadows, and lakesides.

Robinson also offered an opiate for gardeners who spend their small or large fortunes on bedding plants that last but a single season. In his seminal book, *The Wild Garden,* Robinson proposed that gardeners should search the world over for perennial plants that can be adapted to the climate of their own gardens. The perennial border puts an end to the enormous outlay of resources and backbreaking labor involved in planting herbaceous borders of annuals. Robinson realized that native and exotic plants in the Western world are threatened by invasive undesirable wild growing plants. For example, garden pests such as bind weed, Japanese nut weed, and in the Carolinas kudzu and Johnson grass are persistent problems that require substantial resources and labor to control. What Robinson contended several generations ago—plant mainly perennials and develop wild gardens to obviate the need of too much mowing—remains viable today. Even after adjusting for inflation, labor costs more than several generations ago. Moreover it is more difficult than it was several generations ago to find persons willing to stoop, dig, hoe, and do the hard and dirty work required in gardening. Occasional garden labor today can be found at ten dollars, fifteen dollars, or more per hour. Perhaps this is why Emily Whaley always contended that an essential condition of her success as a gardener was "a willing husband with deep pockets."

Robinson's purchase of Gravetye Manor in 1885 gave him the opportunity to put his philosophy of gardening into practice. Robinson's legacy offers a model for us to follow in two respects. First, he superbly incorporated the garden into the vistas from the house. Second, he wisely provided for the conservation of his estate for posterity.

The house at Gravetye was built in 1598 of Sussex limestone from a local quarry. Each of its oak-paneled public areas and bedrooms are filled with three separate sets of eight, over/under, lead glass, and small-paned windows that open onto the garden paradise surrounding the manor. We had the pleasure of staying in Ash, the original master bedroom.

We looked out on the four equal-sized rectangular parterres of Robinson's original plan with an ancient sundial in the stone-paved central axis and walks. To either side were four smaller beds with stone walks. A rectangular pond was featured in the northernmost parterre of the West Garden. Through the lilac-colored columbine vines of our open window to the north, we breathed in the perfume and gazed on the kaleidoscopic colors of enormous clusters of native swamp-azaleas and rhododendron. Robinson's concept of the "wild garden" thus is not incompatible with formal parterres close to the home. Robinson's point was that native wild plants would add much to the formal garden near the home and could be used extensively along walls and in fields too remote for more extensive cultivation. To the south we looked out on a long slope that leads to the trout pond below. That southern slope is the quintessence of Robinson's "wild garden." It was filled with different species of native and exotic foreign wildflowers that come up through the grass and offer diverse colors in the various seasons. The south-slope meadow is mowed and hayed once a year. Our gardener guide, Dave, told us that even toward the end of his life, Robinson would go in his wheelchair along the slope and broadcast thousands of bulbs and seeds onto the meadow for naturalizing.

Robinson lived to be ninety-seven years old, spanning several generations. He took care in his imaginative estate plan to protect Gravetye Manor for future generations. Over the years Robinson had acquired more than one thousand acres adjacent to his manor. On his death most of this acreage was left to the British National Forestry Service. The Gravetye house and acreage was left separately as a leasehold property that could be let by Forestry. After Robinson's death, Gravetye Manor had been used in World War II by the Canadian Armed Forces, and the garden had been allowed to become derelict. In 1957 Peter Herbert came to the rescue of Gravetye Manor and transformed it into the world-famous hotel it now is. The "bones" of Robinson's garden, on which he had lavished fifty years of love and care are still there, so life began again for the Robinson's garden through the heroic efforts of Peter Herbert.

The ambience of Gravetye Manor is magical. The interior is filled with lovely arrangements of flowers from the gardens. Deep-seated sofas surrounding great mantled fireplaces are the final retreat after a masterfully prepared and presented dinner. The formal dining room was a haven of pungent aromas. We feasted on the scallop appetizers and dined on very rare loins of lamb, Dover sole, or roasted breast of corn-fed chicken, served with fresh vegetables from the manor's vegetable garden. Each night we topped off with a dessert of vanilla ice cream and local strawberries.

Our days in the vibrant gardens of Sussex were sunny and warm, but the nights were deliciously cool, a refreshing change from the high 80s temperatures we had left in the Carolina lowcountry. This trip reminded us that when traveling, it is as important to stay in places of great charm and beauty as to visit such places.

During the day families from England, Germany, and France were stretched out on the green velvety lawns in the warm sunshine, enjoying each other's company and the charm of being free from the daily stresses and obligations of life. For me a final walk in the north garden proved an important rule for enjoying a garden: a path must be inviting both coming and going. I wandered down a grass lane toward a huge crimson rhododendron whose borders were planted with crimson primulas. As I turned back, my eye was caught by a white hydrangea surrounded by sweet smelling lilacs. The history, setting, and ambience of Gravetye Manor made it so special that we vowed to return.

If you go:
info@gravetyemanor.co.uk or reception@gravetyemanor.co.uk

Books on or by William Robinson: William Robinson, *The Wild Garden* (an expanded edition with photos and contributions by Rick Darke); Patrick Taylor, *Period Gardens;* Richard Bisgrove, *William Robinson, The Wild Gardener*

Catch these gardens and locations from Gravetye: Scotney Castle, Sheffield Park Estate, Godinton House, Sissinghurst Castle Garden, Great Dixter House and Garden, Hever Castle and Gardens, and Charleston Garden. See Patrick Taylor's *The Garden Lover's Guide to Britain.*

West Dean Gardens and
Lainston House Hotel, England

MAY IN ENGLAND IS A TIME WHEN LILACS BLOOM in a sweet profusion of white, lavender, and purple. We drove across the Sussex Downs from the gardens of West Dean. On the other side of Winchester, we came to Lainston House, a substantial fifty-bedroom brick mansion of the William and Mary era. Our room, "Delft," so named because of its lovely blue and white ceramic tiles, overlooked the terrace and an infinity perspective that reached down a greensward to the light blue hills in the distance. That evening we dined on the terrace as evensong enchanted us with the sounds of doves cooing. An elegant repast began with vichyssoise, followed by halibut and lamb. A bottle of sparkling Italian Prosecco added to the luster of our evening.

We had begun the day at the gardens of West Dean, an expansive landscape in the South Downs, part of the Edward James Foundation. The magnificent house is today a school of the arts. It was designed by James Wyatt (1746–1813) for the First Lord Selsey in 1804. The highlight of our visit included a walk along the great stone-and-flint pergola designed by Harold Peto. The pergola is draped in great profusions of honeysuckle, clematis, and lavender wisteria. At the center of this elegant walk is a charming reflection pool surrounded by hostas.

The five-acre walled garden encloses a Victorian kitchen garden, with much of it in glass houses. We saw the historic development from sunken cold flats to greenhouses filled with espaliered pears, grapes, and figs. Our guide was Shirley Tasker, who had over seven years mastered the art of vegetable growing. She advised that tomatoes, like potatoes, could no longer be grown out of doors in England because of blight. Instead the huge beefsteak tomatoes were growing under glass where they were amply fertilized by horse manure. There was an abundance of fresh peas and beans, with cabbage, Brussels sprouts, and kale grown under nets to protect their luscious fruit from pigeons. Rabbits were kept out by the huge wall of brick. Shirley advised that every third year they refreshed the soil, as they had done this year to keep the raspberries blooming. During the nineteenth century the produce of the garden was so prolific that it was sold at market in London. Today it provides a classic look at a manicured vegetable garden.

We left West Dean Gardens and drove across the green fields of the South Downs. Luminous brilliant-yellow fields of rapeseed alternated with the dark of deep woods, as we drove along our way to Peterfield. It was indeed a day to be out and about in the sunshine and under the blue skies of England. Our destination, Lainston

House, greeted us at dusk. Lainston stands in a huge grove of old pink and white chestnut trees. Three hundred-year-old copper beech trees define the infinity vista. The place has its own vegetable gardens and also raises pork for delicious roasts, sausage, and bacon.

Lainston is probably derived from "Leyne," which means a "farm with a great field" and "Tun" which means an enclosure. Lainston is a sixty-five-acre tract with an ancient high brick-walled garden. The entire tract is unspoiled forest and paths. Our favorite path starts at a cedar barn near the house and goes through gardens down an avenue of massive lime trees planted in 1716. The walk offers superb views as it never strays far from the "infinity" vista of the dining terrace.

In pre-Roman times the Lainston area had been settled by the Belgae, a sophisticated Celtic group who founded the earliest settlement at the site of today's Winchester. From a.d. 85–410 the area became a Roman province. Venta Belgarum (Winchester) was rebuilt in the Roman grid pattern and securely walled. In the late 400s and 500s, a tall, fair Teutonic people migrated to the area from Germany; Cerdic, the leader of these Anglo-Saxon people, founded the kingship of Wessex in 510 and made Winchester its capitol. Queen Elizabeth II is directly descended from Cerdic. During the Dark Ages, the legendary King Arthur governed this area, although the Round Table in the great hall of the Winchester castle was commissioned in the 1500s by Henry VIII. In 802 Egbert of Wessex became supreme over other rulers and is regarded as the father of the English monarchy. From early times Lainston was a part of the Manor of Chilcombe, and all of the English kings prior to the Norman Conquest were crowned at Winchester. William of Normandy was first crowned at Normandy but just to make sure all was in order had himself crowned again in the "royal city" of Winchester. William compiled his *Domesday Book* of 1086 based on King Alfred's *Book of Winchester* and kept these "domes," or laws, in his castle at Winchester. The prehistory of this area reaches back to the time from which the memory of humanity does not reach. We delighted in seeing the megaliths at Stonehenge and the Danbury Ring, both of which lie nearby.

After the Restoration of the monarchy in 1660, Charles II planned a new palace on the ruins of the Winchester Cathedral, and Lainston lay within the adjacent Great Park planned by Christopher Wren. We delighted in the story that Charles II may have brought his lovely mistress Louise Keroualle, duchess of Kent, for dalliances at Lainston. Saying goodbye to a lovely manor house is never easy. But this time it was a promise to return.

If you go: Lainston House, www.lainstonhouse.com; www.westdean.org.uk

Mapperton House, Montacute House, and Barrington Court, England

NEVER UNDERESTIMATE THE TIME IT WILL TAKE to find your destination when driving on English country lanes. From the chalk cliffs on the English Channel to the Quantock Hills at Taunton, Wessex, there is a diverse region of moors and hillsides. We set out one sunny day for the Devon coast in Torquay and the Palace Hotel, a sixty-acre wooded enclave on the "British Riviera." After several hours of driving the narrow roads of the English countryside, we came to Beaminster, where we stopped to visit the house and garden at Mapperton. Near Mapperton, in Somerset, we found another enchanting garden, Barrington Court. The two provide a study in similarities and contrasts.

In 2006 Mapperton had been awarded by *Country Life* magazine the coveted award of Britain's Finest Manor House. Among the criteria for the award is that the house must be occupied residentially (not a museum); have distinguished historic and architectural character; and have a fine setting and contribute to the local life in its community.

Mapperton is one of the oldest Dorset manor houses. It was mentioned in the *Domesday Book* of 1086 as having been the property of the sheriff of Somerset. Remarkably it descended in one family for more than eight hundred years, linked by descent in the female line. The house has medieval origins but was built in the 1540s of local limestone, as was the All Saints Anglican Church, which lies immediately next to it and is now owned by the estate. Many of the tombstones in the graveyard of the church are so ancient that the script of their memorials has been completely effaced by the rains, snows, and winds of yesteryear. The house was remodeled, or, better stated, "evolved" in the 1600s and 1700s. But it is said to "wear the clothes of the 16th, 17th and 18th centuries, as if they all have been designed as one." The house is decorated with massive stone eagles on either side of its entry gates. Its twisting chimney stacks soar above its steep slate roofs. Griffins, lions, and gargoyles stand sentry on its rooftops.

The formal garden dates back to the 1600s, but today's garden is principally the work of Ethel Labouchere (?–1955), who owned the property in the 1920s, and the earl of Sandwich family, who own and occupy the estate today. The garden at Mapperton sits at the top of a steeply descending valley, which winds down to the sea. From the front part of the estate, you would never know there is a garden. We walked slowly to the edge of the croquet lawn at the side of the manor in the direction of the ancient ravine. Suddenly we looked down a terraced slope that must have been part of the original garden. Then an exquisitely designed formal Italian garden sprinkled with a mixture of herbaceous English color was before us. If "surprise" earns points in garden design, the "wow factor" of suddenly looking down onto the Mapperton garden was strikingly evocative.

Anchoring the upper garden is a limestone glass house with nine floor-to-ceiling arched windows accented by four Ionic columns for its larger protruding central section and with Ionic columns in bas relief for each of its side sections. The façade of the glass house turns to a yellow-gold color in the afternoon sun. The central arched window-door was open. We sat for a few minutes soaking in the sun and admiring the grapevines and the fruit on the large pots of limes and lemons. As our eyes glanced forward, we saw the fountain court and its raised pool and fountain. A wisteria-covered pergola lies immediately below the pool on the garden's central, north-south axis. A small summerhouse sits just beyond the pergola, complete with its own fireplace, and offered its artist owner of a century ago shelter from the winter wind. The upper garden is liberally sprinkled with urns, vases, and garden sculpture as focal points.

We looked down on the lower garden from the summerhouse to the two long rectangular pools laid end on end and separated by a small, intermediate circular garden. Both of the pools carry "deep water" warning labels, and they are each long enough for doing swimming laps. Below the lower garden, a stream and bog filled with wildflowers and blooming trees meander down the hill to the sea with grass paths on either side. To our great pleasure, as we walked down the path next to the stream, we were greeted in the adjoining hillside meadow with at least eight or ten brightly colored pheasant cocks and heard a startling mating call. Mapperton today is owned and maintained to perfection by the earl of Sandwich. We had the pleasure of meeting Lady Caroline Sandwich, who takes great care to assure that this lovely Italianate garden continues to thrive in the Wessex countryside.

Returning from Torquay and our stay on the English Riviera, we visited Barrington Court, owned today by the National Trust. Barrington Court was the first property acquired by the National Trust in 1907. The manor house dates from the 1550s and is made from golden Ham Hill stone. The house was leased to Colonel A. A. Lyle from 1920 to 1991. He hired J. E. Forbes, who laid out a garden in compartments in the Arts and Crafts style. Gertrude Jekyll, who was then in her seventies, advised Colonel Lyle on planting the gardens. Today there are three garden rooms that delightfully capture her spirit with flowers and design. The white garden is especially enchanting. The central focal point, a dancing faun, is surrounded by eight beds bursting with white, cream, and silver flowering plants, annuals in the central beds and herbaceous perennials in the outer borders. Another walled enclosure was planted in roses and irises. Wisteria and laburnum were in bloom on the walls, providing a sweet perfume. Inside the manor house we found a special weekend event in progress with local food vendors selling everything from apple cider to sausages and marmalade. We tasted the delicacies and bought a bottle of lemon curd, happy to be a part of a Somerset special event.

If you go: Mapperton Gardens is located two miles southeast of Beaminster and can be reached from the A35 via the B3163. Barrington Court is five miles northeast of Ilminster off the A303. In Torquay we stayed in the Palace Hotel, which has a nine-hole golf course and sits in twenty-six acres of gardens, www.booking.com/palace-hotel-torquay

The garden at Gravetye Manor,
Sussex, England

Left: The author at Dunloe Castle
Hotel, Ireland, with a view of the
Laune River

The Edwardian pond at Bodysgallen, Wales

The knot garden at Bodysgallen, Wales

The Pin Mill at Bodnant
Garden, Wales

Below: A reflecting pond at
Bodnant Garden, Wales

The garden at Powis Castle, Wales

Threave Castle and garden near Galloway, Scotland

Culzean Castle in Maybole, Scotland

Facing, top: The water garden at Threave Castle

Facing, bottom: The walled garden at Culzean Castle, in Maybole, Scotland

Drummond Castle Gardens near Crieff, Scotland

The formal garden at Drummond Castle near Crieff, Scotland

The garden at Levens Hall, near Kendal, England

Newby Hall with colorful herbaceous borders, on the Ure River, Ripon, England

Waddesdon Manor near Aylesbury, England

Facing, top: The water garden at Exbury on the Beaulieu River, in Hampshire, England

Facing, bottom: Henry Hoare's Palladian mansion at Stourhead, near Mere, England

The Pantheon from the Palladian bridge, Stourhead, England

The formal water garden at Danesfield House, Marlowe England

The pergola with wisteria at Chewton Glen in Hampshire, England

The garden at Sharrow Bay in the Lake District, Cumbria, England

Newby Hall, Castle Howard, and Middlethorpe Hall, England

WHAT MAKES ENGLISH GARDENS SO REDOLENT with sweet blooms? Each of us has an answer, including such things as soil, sun and rain, plant selection, and a long tradition of gardening. My answer was found on a bright day in Newby Hall garden in Yorkshire, England. My answer that day was gardeners. At Newby Hall there are seven. Even the owner, Robin Compton, carried a "spade." I had stopped him and asked if he were part of the gardening team. He looked surprised, as I said, "I see you have a shovel." He said, "Madam, in England a shovel is a shovel, but a spade is a spade, and what I have is a spade." He told me his father had laid out the garden, with twenty-five acres of garden on one side of the house and 15 acres of garden on the other.

The design of the garden is influenced by the garden at Hidcote, Gertrude Jekyll's famous garden. The central axis runs from the house down to the Ure River, with magnificent herbaceous borders on either side. Compton had moved the herbaceous borders forward so that the yew hedges behind could be clipped with electric shears. He pointed out the olive-colored weeping pears next to swags of pink roses and said, with a departing flourish, that he had planted them.

Further along I met Malcolm Greaves, a gardener, on both knees weeding. I asked him if weeding were his hardest duty. He replied, "Madam, I am a laborer, and my job is a doodle." When I looked confused, he explained that he had worked on the Compton's sheep ranch and that, compared to that, being a gardener was a cinch.

A lovely lady gardener explained to me that the beds are thirteen feet deep and that the two-foot-high netting stretched over the borders made individual plant staking unnecessary. I asked her whether the borders were mulched when all the perennials were cut back in the fall and was surprised to learn that they had been removing years of built-up mulch as it was preventing much-needed rain from seeping in. The brilliant beds were framed by the yew hedge. At the back were enormous blue delphiniums. Red roses contrasted sharply with the blue of the campanula and the blue of hardy geraniums and mint. Into this salad of blue and green was thrown a dash of yellow achillea.

The entryway to the house was delicious with the scent of lilies and gardenias. The chief flower arranger, Eric Nunn, was arranging a great vase of delphiniums, white lilies, and campanula. Robert Adam (1728–1792) and Thomas Chippendale (1718–1779) had worked together from 1760 to 1772 to create a home of great luxury and taste in Newby Hall. I enjoyed the dining room, where the table was set for ten with a Meissen fruit set. The room, a strong lemon yellow, set off a white plaster frieze with alternating urns and leopard heads. Adam designed four candle-lit alabaster urns for wall niches. The carved doors of oak from Yorkshire with their brass fittings were designed and built by Chippendale.

Our base for the visit to Newby Hall and Castle Howard was Middlethorpe Hall, near the town of York. York is a small, friendly city with a venerable heritage. Middlethorpe Hall is a Georgian estate on the outskirts, in the peaceful community of Bishopthorpe, only a five-minute drive from the center of York. Built in 1699, Middlethorpe is within walking distance of the York racecourse, which holds more than twenty-three weekends of racing events a year. It is a good, country place to stay when visiting one of Britain's most splendid cathedrals, the York Minster. The hotel was salvaged twenty years ago from its life as a nightclub, and today it is a delightful place to enjoy the gardens of Yorkshire, including Newby Hall and Castle Howard.

The gardens of Middlethorpe are luxurious from early spring through late fall. Andrew Leighton, one of two gardeners, shared his gardening expertise with me. Early in March all the grounds are given a good "lifting up," then fertilized with blood and bone, and topped off with mulch from well-filled organic piles. That process gets rid of the weeds and provides the shrubs and perennials the start needed to bloom luxuriantly all year. Early spring brings bulbs and peonies, followed by roses. The walled garden beds are etched with espaliered apples that are used in the kitchen. I noticed bug traps carefully placed under bright green and red apples. Andrew explained that they were pheromone traps designed to catch the male caterpillar with the pungent smell of the female. I noticed that the box hedges had die-back in the center portions. A blight spread by water has been prevalent for the last three years. As Andrew said, "Weather is everything. This year June was perfect with lots of sun, and showers at just the right time." But July came in with daily showers with the results being weeding and mowing at the top of his "to do" list.

After enjoying the walled garden and twenty acres of extensive grounds, I found the swimming pool and workout center. Friendly Yorkshire locals were hard at work getting fit.

We were then off to discover Castle Howard, built in 1700 by Charles, the third earl of Carlisle, and designed in magnificent Baroque style by Sir John Vanbrugh (1664–1726). Vanbrugh was a playwright with great flair and imagination. The central domed entry hall stands seventy feet high with encircling steps. An Italian, Antonio Pelligrini (1675–1741), did the elaborate murals on the domed ceiling. Vanbrugh and the third earl had met each other at the Kit-Cat Club, where members included the duke of Marlborough, Sir Robert Walpole, and the writers Congreve,

Addison, and Steele. The dramatic castle is stilled lived in by the family. The ambience of Castle Howard was vibrant with a jazz band playing and groups of musicians gathered in the sun on the green.

Breakfast the next morning at Middlethorpe included two soft-poached eggs with mushrooms, potatoes, and smoked salmon. All the bread is baked locally, and the croissants were light and fluffy and accompanied by orange marmalade. We enjoyed coffee and hot chocolate in one of the sitting rooms where the walls were adorned by eight Giovanni Piranesi (1720–1778) engravings of Italy. Other walls had elegant portraits and handsome oil landscapes. The total effect was of relaxed dignity.

Yorkshire, with its country estates, exquisite gardens and great central city is like getting back into the mid-1900s South Carolina lowcountry dominated by plantations such as Middleton, Mulberry, and Mepkin. Short of having a family own and occupy this ancestral home, Middlethorpe Hall has been put to its highest and best conservative economic use as a guest house. York and Middlethorpe are easily reached through the Manchester airport. This airport also provides access to all of Wales and Scotland. It is easy-in and easy-out, which in today's hectic travel world is a big plus.

If you go:
www.middlethorpe.com (Tel. 01904 641241); Castle Howard, 14 miles
NE of York by the A64; Newby Hall, 4 miles SE of Ripon on the B6265,
www.newbyhall.com

The best book as a guide to gardens in England, Scotland, and Wales is Patrick Taylor's *The Garden Lover's Guide to Britain.*

Levens Hall and Sharrow Bay Hotel, England

LEVENS HALL, IN THE LAKE DISTRICT OF ENGLAND, is a house and garden with a seventeeth-century feel. We entered Levens through a gate and were amazed by the flock of Bagot goats with their brown necks and faces. The gardens merge imperceptibly with the surrounding pastures, protected from the grazing herds of brown cows by a moat called a haw-haw. The yew and box topiary was designed in 1694 by Guillaume Beaumont, a French horticulturist. The topiary is pruned in such shapes as umbrellas, chess pieces, a jug, and peacocks. The gardener told me that it takes four men six months to clip and maintain the topiary garden. Beech hedges form the wall around the garden and are espaliered over arbors providing welcoming shade.

Somehow my nose always leads me to the rose garden. I stood on one side of the rose parterres with a light breeze wafting the sweet lemony aroma of hundreds of David Austin roses. These roses showed not a sign of spray or of having brown spot or mildew. The secret is the selection of the most disease-resistant of the Austin species. Each rose was labeled and varieties included Belle Story, Perdita, Gertrude Jekyll, Mary Rose, and Wife of Bath, all in shades of pink. All soil had been replaced when these repeat blooming roses had been planted, to prevent soil-borne disease.

The house at Levens is from the sixteenth century. Each room is paneled in oak with detailed plaster ceilings. Windows are of leaded glass often with small coats-of-arms inset in stained glass. Throughout the house huge fireplaces have intricately carved oak over-mantels. I noticed that there was a magnificent working clock in each room. We learned that the owner collected clocks. So it came as no surprise when suddenly the house sang with chimes tolling the hour of three.

Our base for exploring Cumbria and the Lake District was Sharrow Bay on the Ullswater. This elegant and welcoming retreat is an ideal spot for visiting Levens Hall. Sun-speckled green pastures, sheep bleated, and hawks soared as I walked through the green fields near the Sharrow Bay Country House Hotel. On a July day the temperature was in the mid-60s, and a cool breeze was blowing off the glacier-made lake. My purpose was to learn a "wee" bit about sheep farming. I stopped two sturdy men walking my way, Robert Hawkings and his assistant, Phil. They were headed to Sharrow Bay Hotel, where they maintain the lovely gardens. Robert told me that no ewe is happy unless she has a set of two lambs. The lambs are born in

January, and by August of each year they are turned into succulent lamb for the table. The rams with their curling horns are kept separately until the time is ripe for more young. I felt an uncomfortable rumble in my tummy, having dined on delicate and rare lamb the night before.

Robert invited me to his garden, an enclave surrounded by high yew hedges with roses, dahlias, fuchsias, snapdragons, and a myriad of stunning focal points. My favorite was a marble David. Sharrow Bay Hotel is a family enterprise. Robert's friend Phil was busy in the hotel, changing out the brilliant pots of begonias that brighten each room. His wife, Jenny, comes in twice a week to create colorful flower arrangements for the four comfortable sitting rooms. His cat Sam, who was stretching among the dahlias, greets him each morning at the garden gate.

The hotel was founded in 1948 by Francis Coulson, whose passion for collecting is visible in every room. Meissen clocks and statues adorn each mantel. Lighted and mirrored glass cabinets contain English porcelains and Bohemian glass in shades of pink, lavender, and green. A gentleman visitor advised me that this was his fiftieth year of coming for weekend retreats to Sharrow Bay.

The dining room overlooks the lake with a view of yachts and sailboats with spinnakers flying in the stiff breeze. Our table was in a mirrored alcove with a full window vista of the moving clouds and waves. Breakfast was served elegantly, prepared by the second in command, Chef Marc Teasdale. When I visited his kitchen, he was setting two loaves of walnut and currant brown bread into a hot oven, in anticipation of lunch. Breakfast began with hot milk and coffee, with their specially prepared muesli. There were poached eggs, black pudding, and delicious ham and bacon. There was no holding back, as each of the treats was delicious, tender, and mouth watering. Dinner that evening was an elegant repast, beautifully served by a team of Hungarian waiters. We began with avocado and shrimp appetizers in the drawing room. When seated, we enjoyed crab salad served with a fresh pineapple garnish. The main course featured a choice of tender lamb garnished with a chutney sauce or fresh sea bass on spinach and potatoes. Dessert was a raspberry tart with custard. We declined the cheese course and found our charming bedroom, all outfitted in blue and yellow curtains and bed hangings. Earlier in the day, we had watched Tom Watson bring a touch of nostalgia and a swell of glory into the hearts of every senior golfer in the world at the British Open in Turnberry. But alas, later that night, it was not to be.

Sharrow Bay on the Ullswater is a perfect destination for visiting England's Lake District. Formed during the Ice Age, about ten thousand years ago, the lakes were chiseled out by retreating glaciers. The Ullswater is an especially appealing lake that appears both blue and gray, depending on the clouds, the shadows, and the encompassing mountains. On our last day it was deep blue, with a red and blue sailboat skimming the waves. I asked, "Why leave?" But I have an old saying, "Never look back, and always expect that tomorrow will be as engaging as today."

If you go: Sharrow Bay Country Hotel is easily reached in about two hours from the Manchester Airport. It can be found on the Internet at www.sharrow.co.uk (Tel. 44(0) 1768 486301). Levens Hall is five miles south of Kendal by the A591.

Edinburgh and Prestonfield House, Scotland

A Base for Discovering the Borders

SCOTLAND FASCINATES AMERICANS. It is a heritage that includes men wearing kilts, the male bonding of the haggis ceremony, and the eerie lilt of song and bagpipe. It is also a country that bursts with beautiful gardens, verdant golf courses, and vintage castles.

We left Charleston on a hot July day; our destination was the city of Edinburgh. It provides a perfect base for visiting the border region south of the city, as well as the east coast on the Firth of Forth. Our home away from home was Prestonfield House. Prestonfield sits on the edge of Holyrood Park, an immense hillock in the middle of Edinburgh. It is an old and imposing white mansion with a restaurant, Rhubarb, that has an outstanding reputation. Prestonfield has a country feeling in the middle of a big city. Each day we walked the loop around Holyrood (a four-mile walk), and once we ventured up the steep hillside to Arthur's Seat, the presumed throne of King Arthur. The Prestonfield golf links were directly below our window. The unwary golfer with a great shot was amazed to hear a voice from on high applauding his skill. The par 70 course of 6,207 yards was designed by James Braid and overlooks Duddingston Loch. There were ten peacocks on the grounds whose screams were enough to arouse one from any dream.

The greatest treat was breakfast at Rhubarb. A huge feast of fresh fruit, scrambled or poached eggs, black pudding, sausage, and delicious mushrooms awaited us. The portraits that lined the dining room lent an air of solemnity to the occasion. Benjamin Franklin once stayed here and is said to have commented, "The hospitality was beyond compare, and even the bed bugs don't bite." Prestonfield House was built in 1687 by William Bruce (c. 1630–1710). Today it has been spruced up by James Thompson, who also owns the Whitchery by the Castle, a sumptuous restaurant on the Royal Mile.

To our great surprise, Fred's cousin Effie Siegling Bowers arrived at Prestonfield with a group from the British National Trust. Effie had grown up in the stately and historic Siegling home at High Battery, overlooking Charleston Harbor and Fort Sumter, a home today owned by Richard Jenrette. What a great pleasure it was to chance upon another Charlestonian in Scotland and family at that. We enjoyed a long breakfast with Effie the next morning at Rhubarb Restaurant, punctuated by spirited conversation and reminiscences.

Our first destination was the town of Peeble in the Borders region. It is filled with small shops and bustling townspeople. We lunched just outside the town in the Cringletie House Hotel. I felt as though I were in my grandmother's house. There was a wonderful coal fire in the grate and a cozy bar with magazines. I walked on the twenty-eight acres of woodlands that were filled with long-horned Highland cattle and black-faced sheep. The manager, Jeremy Osborne, was anxious to arrange fishing on the Tweed or shooting of partridges and pheasants. He was disappointed that all I wanted to do was walk in his lovely walled garden, where I found gooseberries, strawberries, rhubarb, onions, and tomatoes as well as the darting of swallows and the cawing of crows.

From Cringletie we visited Kalzie Garden, privately owned by Lady Hepburn. Her gardener, Guy Crowhurst, had his dog Sam with him to chase down the pesky rabbits. Roses were intertwined with clematis. He attributed the huge blooms to tons of well-rotted cow manure. The silver weeping pears provided corner focal points. In all there were three acres within this old walled garden. Rambling through it all by ourselves, we were mesmerized by the sweet smells of roses, lavender, and honeysuckle.

We left Kalzie Garden to visit Melrose Abbey, where pink ruins dominate the surrounding landscape. Sir Walter Scott said, "If thou would'st view fair Melrose aright, Go visit it by the pale moonlight. For the gay beams of lightsome day; Gild, but to flout the ruins grey. . . ." I was startled to discover the legend that the Cistercian monks practiced the removal of the heart from the body for burial and that Robert the Bruce's heart is buried at Melrose Abbey. On a lighter note, we visited two lovely National Trust of Scotland gardens, Harmony and Priorwood, the vistas of which are through apple and pear trees to the abbey ruins. Priorwood is known as a center for drying flowers from peonies to lupines.

We woke up back at Prestonfield House, singing "Somewhere over the Rainbow," and jauntily set out for East Lothian and its blue, blue skies. That land was the lovely town of Gullane on the Firth of Forth and Greywalls, a famed hotel overlooking the Muirfield golf course. We were welcomed by the owner, Ros Weaver, whose family has owned the house/hotel since the 1940s. Designed in 1901 by the famous Edwardian architect Sir Edwin Lutyens (1869–1944), the house has the ambience of South Carolina's old plantation homes. We settled onto the terrace to enjoy cocktails and watch the golfers tee off. Lunch was in a cozy room overlooking the tenth tee at Muirfield. We had delicious fresh salmon with tiny green beans and a pungent sauce. The chef, David Williams, delights in using local produce.

Finding Greywalls was like finding a pearl in an oyster shell. The tranquility and the Old World charm and style provided an intense sense of security and freedom from all cares. I toured the garden with Ros Weaver as she pointed out her secrets of success. This year everything had bloomed at once. White peonies were nodding next to white hydrangeas in beds edged with dusty miller, santolina, and lambs' ears. Bright-orange poppies followed Gertrude Jekyll's maxim of putting hot colors in the middle. We ventured down the herbaceous border that was flowing over its borders with blue delphiniums, blue lupines, and hardy purple and mauve geraniums.

Our second-floor room looked down on the principal garden and back to a stone wall with a large circular opening with a vista onto the moor. We were excited to learn that our lovely room had served as quarters for Arnold Palmer when he won the British Open at Muirfield.

When traveling we are always quite optimistic, anticipating the next arrival and hoping that the best is yet to come. Indeed the best was yet to come, as our final destination was home, lovely Charleston with its welcoming sea breezes.

If you go:
Cringletie House Hotel, www.cringletie.com

PrestonfieldHotel, www.prestonfield.com

www.greywalls.co.uk

Broughton House, Culzean Castle, and Hill House, Scotland

OUR TRIP BEGAN IN BEAUTIFUL GALLOWAY at Kirkcudbright, where we stayed at the Selkirk Arms. Gusty winds, downpours, black skies, and a penetrating cold had blown in from the sea. The inn had a bright coal fire, and in June! The next day in sunnier weather we toured lovely Broughton House, the home of the Scottish artist Edward Atkinson Hornel (1864–1933). Newly restored by the National Trust for Scotland, the house has become a center for the study of both Hornel and the Scottish poet Robert (Rabbie) Burns (1759–1796).

Jim Allen, a librarian employed by the National Trust, gave us a special tour, proudly noting that there were more than twenty-five hundred unique titles on Burns in a collection of over fifteen thousand volumes. The books jostled for attention with the magical paintings of Hornel.

Jim wondered if I could recite the "Selkirk" grace, written by Burns many years ago at our hotel, the Selkirk Arms. To his delight, I began: "Some have meat, and cannot eat, And some cannot eat that want it; But we have meat, and we can eat— And let the Lord be thanked." I knew it, as my grandmother Anne Sinkler Fishburne, of Scottish descent and a Burns fan, always quoted it for Sunday grace at her table in Pinopolis, South Carolina.

Broughton House was filled with paintings and portraits by the many artists who had lived in Kircudbright in the 1880s. Hornel had traveled widely to Japan, Ceylon, Australia, Singapore, and Hong Kong. His studio held many of his late paintings of young girls gamboling in meadows. One painting showed an eerie spirit in gray, peeking from dense Scottish woods. I was entranced by one huge wall-hanging in bright greens, blues, and reds, a dramatic scene of a Samurai warrior with a huge knife, defending a Japanese woman. Hornel had brought the large wall-hanging back from his 1893 trip to Japan.

A lovely garden that extends to the Dee River beckoned. It progresses in a series of small rooms, each with its sundial (including the night hours as the sun does not set until 10 P.M. in summer). Each "sitting room" is edged carefully in miniature box. I especially relished the colorful combination of featherweight mauve poppies and fragrant "Bowl of Beauty" pink peonies. The gray stone walls are embossed with climbing white lace-cap hydrangeas intertwined with purple clematis.

The next two days provided a unique chance to compare houses designed and decorated by two of Scotland's top architects. In 1776 Robert Adam (1728–1792) was hired by David Kennedy, the tenth earl of Cassillis (1727–1792) to improve and redesign the family mansion at Culzean, near present-day Turnberry in Ayrshire. Both men had been on the Grand Tour, where they immersed themselves in the classical world, visiting galleries, churches, and sites that evoked the world of Greece and Rome. In Culzean Castle, Adam created a synthesis of architecture, planning, and decoration, rich in the classical motif. The library epitomizes the Adam style. The ceiling has three painted stucco roundels of beautiful dancing girls, while the ceiling frieze has motifs of fruit and vines. Adam designed the fireplace mantel in pure white Carrara marble, and its delicate ornaments echo those of the frieze and door entablature. The castle holds a commanding position over the sea with six hundred acres of surrounding woodland. It is possible to book a room in Culzean and walk the ramparts as dusk falls. On a later trip to Culzean, we had the pleasure of staying in the "Eisenhower suite" on the top floor of the castle. Knowing Ike's love for golf, the Culzean owners had gratefully deeded a life estate in the top floor of the castle to Eisenhower for serving as Allied commander so he could play golf at Turnberry.

The walled garden at Culzean has a series of deep herbaceous borders. Ian, the chief gardener, said the bees were a "wee bit vigorous" and "anything blue, the bees go to." Starting with blue campanula and purple delphiniums at the back, the border includes lupines, yarrow, phlox, shasta daisies, veronicas, and masses of blue pelargonium. Poppies and peonies fill borders abutting the walls. The walled garden, begun in 1775, is lined with bricks to hold heat. We spent two nights near Culzean at the Malin Court, which abuts the Kyntire golf course. On a hillside above the Firth of Clyde, we watched glorious sunsets.

From Ayrshire we traveled north to Hill House, designed by Charles Rennie Mackintosh (1868–1928) with the assistance of his wife Margaret. Just north of Glasgow on a high hill, the turreted stucco house sits in a garden with views over the Clyde River. Mackintosh's use of a restrained color palette joins with the repeated architectural elements of the square and rectangle to give the house interior a minimalist effect. These elements are repeated in light fixtures, leaded-glass windows, ornaments, furniture, and wall hangings. The drawing room, with its brightly lit alcove of windows, contains a gesso panel by Margaret MacDonald Mackintosh (1865–1933) that illustrates the story of Sleeping Beauty. The girl in gold, covered with stylized pink roses, slumbers enmeshed in protective coils of briers, impenetrable to all but the bravest suitor. Margaret's evocative paintings throughout the house show a remarkable similarity to those of Gustav Klimt (1862–1918). The McDonalds had been friends with Klimt during a prior residence on the continent. The Sleeping Beauty fable is a perfect metaphor for Hill House. Constructed in 1903, the house had lain "asleep" for a century when the National Trust of Scotland provided the "kiss" that brought her back to life.

A perfect base for exploring the lowlands of Scotland is Glenapp Castle at Ballantrae. The castle was built in 1870 for James Hunter by the renowned architect David Bryce (1803–1876). Its present iteration as an elegant hotel stems from its acquisition in 1994 by Graham and Fay Cowan. Fay's father founded the McMilan Hotel group of seven country houses. Glenapp had become derelict by the time Graham and Fay took on the task of restoring it in 1994, and workmen had to labor six days a week for six years to redo the plumbing and electricity and turn the castle into a cozy, inviting destination. Today, thanks to Fay's way with style, it is an emporium of beautiful paintings, statues, and comfortable sitting rooms. Ceilings are elegantly plastered, while Adam-style mantels are decorated with period clocks, all ticking away in perfect time.

We discovered this charming estate while looking for a base to visit the lowland gardens of Threave, Culzean Castle, and Castle Kennedy and for a location for playing golf at the famed British Open course at Turnberry. How fabulous to discover that Glenapp comprised all the essentials of a Scottish lowland garden. Anne Marie Mitchell, a garden consultant with gritty fingers, has brought the garden back into its a glorious state. She showed me her pictures of an abandoned, overgrown walled garden with a disintegrating glass house. She told me that this garden had been a great challenge for her and gave her a chance to become a head gardener. Her garden career began with her working as an apprentice at Threave, and she went on from there to Logan Botanic Garden. When she announced to her mentor at Logan that she was leaving to become the head gardener at Glenapp, he erupted, "How could you possibly leave? You are our very best weeder!"

I knew that dinner was in the offing when I saw Eric, a local Scottish fisherman, drive in the back way with a load of local lobster and crab. The head chef, Adam Stokes, a tall lad of only twenty-eight, provided a magnificent six-course dinner, appropriately sized and tempting. Each of his plates looked like a painting, with dainty sauces outlining the choice morsels. A green swathe of petit pois surrounded the lobster tail, while the crab was in an elegant orange chimney. The choice of main course was young spring lamb in a rosemary and wine sauce or a filet of Cairnhill Farm beef with truffles and foie gras, braised onions, and a red wine sauce. Dessert was a choice of Glenapp strawberries and cream with champagne jelly, or Scottish Cranashan soufflé with raspberry sorbet. My answer was no to the cheese tray, and no to the coffee, but yes to all the other treats.

Each day in Scotland brought some rain, some blustery wind, and blue sky with glinting sun. But as a wise Scotsman advised me, "Madam, you don't come to Scotland for the weather!" I watched the sea turn alternately green, silver, white, and blue before I headed back to Glenapp for another feast.

If you go:
www.glenappcastle.com

Selkirk Arms Hotel, Kirkcudbright (Fax 01557 331693),
www.selkirkarmshotel.co.uk

Malin Court, Turnberry, Ayrshire, www.malincourt.co.uk

Broughton House, Kirkcudbright

Culzean Castle, Maypole, KA198LE (Fax 0044 (0)1655 884503),
culzeanexperience.org. There are four suites on the top floor at Culzean,
and all areas are available for reservations.

Hill House, Helensburg, Scotland, www.hillhouse.co.uk

July Gardens in Scotland

TRAVELERS ABROAD ARE HOPING FOR INSPIRATION. I am always looking for gardening tips that I can incorporate into my own garden, which sits on a hillside peninsula at Lake Summit, in Tuxedo, North Carolina. Whether it is an old-fashioned patterned garden, an Arts and Crafts walled garden, a landscape garden. or an outdoor decorator's garden room, the inspiration stirred by seeing another style of garden ignites my imagination.

Scotland in July is magic. Daylight begins at 4 A.M. and lasts until 11 P.M. Expansive light creates a spectrum from the soft glow of morning, to the stark clarity of midday, to evening shadows that merge into bold sunsets of gold, yellow, and purple. Proximity to the Gulf Stream, long summer days, and abundant rainfall provide perfect gardening conditions.

The west coast of Scotland, whose rainfall can total more than 80 inches per year, benefits from the balmy effects of the Gulf Stream. Gardens such as those at Threave, Culzean Castle, and Torosay Castle abound in tender plants collected from the Himalayas, New Zealand, Chile, and South Africa. Plant collectors who ventured to the furthermost reaches of the British Empire brought home Himalayan rhododendrons with fragrant blooms, New Zealand cabbage palms, Chilean lobelias, tree ferns, and Australian eucalyptus. Plunging into these garden landscapes is a visit into the world of exotic and rare plants.

Threave Castle and garden are located in Galloway near the small Atlantic town of Kirkcudbright. Threave is an example of the multitype garden, in that on this vast estate there are gardens of every type: walled, water, and formal. Threave is owned by the National Trust of Scotland. The sunny, bright day we visited Threave, we met Bob Browne, the chief gardener, who told us that he had worked in this garden for forty years. He gave us some of his secret tips: dig dahlias in September after the first killing frost and store them upside down for the winter so that the bulbs will not hold water; plant marigolds in rows between lettuce; separate currants and blackberries with dahlias; use loads of cow manure and till it in well. The water garden was filled with damp-loving aquatic plants including iris, primula, and waterlily. We spent the night nearby at the Selkirk Arms in Kirkcudbright. The bar in the inn was full of locals talking and drinking single-malt scotch or pale ale.

Scotland is a country of islands. The island of Mull in the Inner Hebrides is one of its most beautiful. We purchased tickets on the Caledonia ferry from Oban to Mull. There we found Torosay Castle and Garden. The castle, dating from 1858 and in the Scottish Baronial style, was designed by a leading Victorian architect, David Bryce. Robert Lorimer (1864–1929) created the design for the Torosay garden. This is a formal garden in the Italianate style, where terraces, balustrades, and ornaments provide a structured framework. Breathtaking vistas of green hills and blue waters link the garden to its surrounding countryside. Sir Winston Churchill was often a guest here, and the house maintains the record of his hunting prowess. When we returned to the Caledonian Hotel in Oban, we were treated to a bevy of beautiful Scottish lasses doing the traditional sword dance.

It was difficult saying goodbye to the west coast of Scotland with its beautiful views over the ocean. However, Fife and central Scotland beckoned. The castle gardens of Fife are an excursion into the inventive and lively world of color. Such gardens as those at Drummond Castle, Kellie Castle, and Kinross House have brilliant herbaceous borders with dazzling mixtures of perennials, roses, and bulbs.

Drummond Castle Gardens is near Crieff in Perthshire. This is a patterned garden designed for lavish display of bedding plants. The drive to the castle is through a narrow avenue of beech and lime trees, flanked by rural farmland. Visitors enter a courtyard behind the fifteenth-century castle. There is no sign of the garden, which is hidden behind a low wall. With delightful impact this nineteenth-century Victorian garden reveals itself suddenly, completely, and startlingly. There, all at once in the valley below, is a gigantic thirteen-acre parterre in the shape of a St. Andrews cross. The present garden was begun in 1838 and was completed in 1842 in time for a visit by Queen Victoria. On the day we visited, four full-time gardeners were busy clipping, planting, and maintaining this huge garden and its ornaments.

We headed to Dunblane and visited the extraordinary twelfth-century Gothic cathedral. While there, we stayed at the Dunblane Hydro Hotel, which has a superb indoor swimming pool. Our garden destination was Kinross House and its garden in the town of Kinross, about twenty-five miles north of Edinburgh. Kinross is an example of a formal garden with an all-at-once design. House and garden were conceived together and begun in 1679. The garden is enclosed by an ancient wall that is pierced by roundels and wrought-iron gates. Through the gate there is a marvelous eye-catcher, the ruin of Loch Leven Castle, on an island in the lake. The castle view links the garden to the countryside. This castle was where Mary, Queen of Scots, was imprisoned in 1567. A central water fountain strengthens the formal garden design, and this is a garden for roses of all types. Climbing roses adorn the walls, while pink David Austin roses grace the geometric beds. We visited Kinross garden on a misty, rainy day and were totally alone in the quiet of this peaceful place.

We visited Kellie Castle on a sunny, bluebird day. Before we left, rain showers made us happy to have an umbrella. Kellie Castle and garden invoked images of Sleeping Beauty, much as Hill House had done earlier. Imagine a castle tower from the thirteenth century surrounded by a high stone wall smothered in climbing pink roses and lavender clematis. Inside the wall, shaven green lawns and paths separate deep borders filled with sweet-smelling roses. The garden was designed by Robert Lorimer, a famous Scottish architect, and is an example of an Arts and Crafts garden. Lorimer described his vision of the perfect garden: "Great intersecting walks of shaven grass, on either side borders of brightest flowers backed up by low espaliers hanging with shining apples."

Scotland rings with our Celtic heritage. This closing bit of Robert Burns seems attuned to our visit.

> O were my Love yon lilac fair,
>   Wi' purple blossoms to the spring,
> And I a bird to shelter there,
>   When wearied on my little wing.

If you go:

Selkirk Arms Hotel, reception@selkirkarmshotel.co.uk

Dunblane Hydro Hotel, www.hilton.com/dunblanehydro

Caledonian Hotel, Oban (Tel. 08448559135)

See also www.historic-scotland.gov.uk.

Patrick Taylor's *The Garden Lover's Guide to Britain* contains a superb chapter that includes all of these gardens in Scotland. Another worthwhile guide is Francesca Greenoak's *The Gardens of the National Trust for Scotland.*

"Oh, My Ireland of Dreams!"

MEMORIES OF IRELAND FUELED THE EXPLOSION of nostalgic songs that tell of American Irish yearning for their homeland. Hum along to the tune of "Methuselah": "Methuselah, Methuselah, your warm arms are saying that death is a dream and love is forever . . ."; or sing Danny Boy, "Oh, Danny boy, the pipes, the pipes are calling . . ."; or thrill to the high notes of tenor John McCormick trilling "But a lad of eighteen summers, still there's no one can deny, as he walked to death that morning, he proudly held his head on high." Or remember the stories of fairies, leprechauns, and banshees from our grandmothers.

Ireland in June is verdant with lush flowers and a luminous green from trees and grass. The song of the wind at times is purring and at other times growling. The weather is quixotic, one moment brilliant, hot, and sunny, and the next blustery, with scudding gray, rain-filled clouds. The paradox of the Irish character may be explained by this intensely changing scene and the people's struggle for freedom from the British.

We set out in June to see the gardens of southern Ireland, and there we found the beautiful gardens of Kerry and Cork. Killarney is the perfect base, as it sits on the edge of the Ring of Kerry, in the midst of three lovely lakes. The scenery is dramatic with green and blue mountains that are gushing with sun-glinted waterfalls. The Gap of Dunloe forms the perfect "V" between these verdant peaks.

Our first destination was Dunloe Castle Hotel. Today, a superb five-star hotel, it provides an array of athletic endeavors, including fly-fishing on the Laune River and hiking up to the Gap of Dunloe. The castle was built in 1213 and could well have been the home of Rapunzel with its high, unreachable windows. The garden dates from 1922, when Howard Harrington, a well-to-do American, decided to build a home and garden with a magnificent panoramic view of the towering Macgillycuddy's Reeks. There are huge old trees including a purple beech, a hornbeam from Asia, a hazel, Chinese cherry trees, and rare maples. The blooms of sweet-scented white rhododendron attract bees, and pink azaleas dot woodland paths. The river Laune was framed by a hillside of pink hydrangeas. I sat and watched a gentleman equipped with three fly rods try for a big salmon in the Laune. That evening I dined on a succulent portion of salmon from the Laune, topped with onions in a white-wine sauce and nestled in a bed of white asparagus and potatoes. There was Irish music lilting from a piano, and, yes, there was "A tear in my eye, and I'm wondering why."

We decided to chance the excitement of a trip along the Ring of Kerry. Each bend in the narrow road brought a surprise. Our first stop was Muckross House, where the chief gardener, Patrick Murphy, showed us through the glass houses, one from 1890 built in Dublin. He was proud of his black geranium and towering bird of paradise. A tour of Muckross House, dating from 1843, was a trip back into long-ago times. The family living there had spent so much restoring the house for Queen Victoria's visit that it was bankrupted. So much for royal visits! Each window presented incredible views of landscaped gardens and Muckross Lake.

Our way around the Ring of Kerry took us up over Moll's Gap through stunning scenery of cliffs, mountains and lakes. We came down into the town of Kenmare, where green, pink, blue, and yellow shops line the central square. We browsed for fine woolens and stocked up on cheese for the drinking hour. Our destination on Bantry Bay, a wind-whipped arm of the sea, was Bantry House. This eighteenth-century stately home is owned by Egerton White, the ninth generation "laird" of this manor. The original Queen Anne house (stone with red-brick accents) was built in 1700. We stayed for two nights in the east wing, with a magnificent view of the gardens and the sea, and enjoyed playing billiards in front of a glowing coal fire. We wandered around the house at twilight, discovering treasures: the 1770 rose-colored tapestry thought to have been made for Marie Antoinette for her marriage to the dauphin of France; the portraits of King George II by Allan Ramsay; walls filled with eighteenth-century engravings by Piranesi and Tiepolo; and from Italy hand-carved Cararra marble fireplaces with goddesses standing on seashells in bas-relief. The chief gardener, Lorna Finnegan, took me around the garden, explaining the axial layout of terracing, balustrades, statuary, and parterres, as well as the hundred steps to the sky behind the house. I sat on the top step in the gloaming, watching the sailboats on Bantry Bay. My favorite memory of this fabulous place is the statue of Diana with her quiver and a fawn at the entry portal. Breakfast at Bantry House, with Anne and Marie in the kitchen, was a hearty feast of soft-poached eggs, ham, brown toast, yogurt mixed with raspberries, and strong coffee. We left Bantry House as our host, the earl of White (on a rider mower) was clipping his lawns in anticipation of hosting the eleventh West Cork Chamber Music Festival.

We found our way north to the Shannon River and Glin Castle. "Where dear old Shannon's flowing, where the three-leaved shamrocks grow, where my heart is, I am going. . . ." The Shannon is a tidal estuary whose blue and green, white-capped waters were glinting under a bright sun. The house nestles in the hills and dates from the 1780s. It has been owned for the past seven centuries by the Knights of Glin. The walled garden of Glin was full of vegetables for the table. The gray stone walls of the garden support espaliered figs, apples, and pears, and the blue and mauve of hardy geraniums surround a sunny seating nook. Our room had three magnificent windows overlooking the formal garden, and its walls were lined with old prints and engravings, vintage porcelain, and oil paintings. Dinner in the elegant portrait-lined dining room was a treat. We began with drinks before a fire. A friendly lawyer from Los Angeles played a medley of "East Side, West Side," and "It's a Long Way to Tipperary." That evening we dined on scallops and leeks surrounding fresh salmon, a fresh spinach soup, local fish, and succulent lamb. "May you always have a sunbeam to warm you" is an old Irish saying that is oh so true. Every day in Ireland brings some sun, some rain, some fog, and rising dews.

We had arrived in Shannon, and so a fitting departure was Dublin, the home of Swift, Yeats, Beckett, and Behan, who sang: "There's no place on earth like the world, there's no place that I'd rather be!" We toured the National Gallery of Ireland, enjoying the landscapes by Nathaniel Holme and James A. O'Connor. We enjoyed the Georgian yellow, blue, and red front doors, which, as a guard said, are "like a man's bow tie."

We laughed at the Irish sense of humor, wherever we went. I asked two handsome, well-dressed young men what they did for a living. They responded, "We're in the doom and gloom business, and when we solve it, we will come to the USA, and help you." They were bankers. We asked a lady at breakfast about her life. She sighed that her life was overwhelmed with children who would not fly the coop. She said, "We have had to sell our house to get rid of our grown children!" I asked a handsome man in a silk suit, tie, and shirt with gold cuffs to show me the way to Grafton Street for shopping. I asked further if he were an attorney. He responded, "No, I am not; I am completely normal!" We laughed our way home to Hunter's Inn, an old coaching inn in the countryside from Dublin. At breakfast I met Hayden Doyle, chief of the Plasterers Union of Ireland. He had a twinkle in his eye. Breaking a cardinal rule of my mother, Emily Whaley ("Never talk politics or religion"), I asked him what he thought of the "good" done for Ireland by the European Union. He responded in a thick Irish brogue: "Why my lass, I have had to hire ten translators since 2004. These Poles, Slovakians, and Russians will work for nothing and sleep in their cars."

We did one more round of gardens before leaving Ireland. Just south of Dublin we visited both Powerscourt and Killruddery. We were totally by ourselves at Killrudddery, a wonderful French-style garden with two magnificent reflection canals. The gardens date from 1682. We especially loved the conservatory, a glassed-in enclosure filled with superb marble statuary. We then drove only ten minutes to Powerscourt, a superb Italian-style garden. The house has been turned into a shopping arcade, but the gardens sing with style, design, flowers, and vistas.

We left Ireland for Wales, smiling and rhyming the words of an old Irish blessing: "Laughter to cheer you, faithful friends near you, and whenever you pray, for Heaven to hear you!"

If you go:

Killarney, Hotel Dunloe Castle, www.thedunloe.com (Tel. 353-64-66-44111)

Killarney, Hotel Europe, www.killarneyhotels.ie (Tel. 064 71350)

Bantry House, www.bantryhouse.ie (Tel. 027 50047)

Glin Castle, www.glincastle.com (Tel. 068 34173)

Hunter's Hotel, www.hunters.ie (Tel. 040 40106)

To read: Terrence Reeves-Smyth, *The Garden Lover's Guide to Ireland*

The best time of the year to visit Ireland is April–May or August–September.

Bodysgallen, Bodnant, and Powis Castle, Wales

JUST WHEN I FEEL THAT I HAVE LEARNED all there is to know about the English language, I come upon Welsh, where "ll" is pronounced as a "cl." Wales is unique, with its ancient flavorful Celtic language, sympathetic and friendly people, and rolling, sheep-filled green pastures. Like the Scots, the Welsh, in modern times, have been able to obtain their own Parliament with power over local issues such as language. All road signs are in Welsh as well as English.

Bodysgallen, our base for visiting castles and gardens in northern Wales, is a beautifully restored seventeenth-century castle. The atmosphere is elegant, yet home-like. There are three comfortable sitting rooms, each with lovely old portraits, deep sofas, and guests enjoying the luxury of reading, chatting, or meditating. Break-fast was a treat with its black pudding, eggs, stewed tomatoes, mushrooms, bacon, and sausage. At our first luncheon we met an attractive, well-to-do couple, who had arrived in their private helicopter for the day to celebrate her birthday. When I asked him how he liked Prime Minister Brown, he responded, "You should know the answer; he should put on the uniform and lead our troops in Afghanistan." My spouse quietly kicked me under the table, and I again remembered my mother's words, "Never talk politics or religion." Later he invited us to visit his garden near Chatsworth and offered to bring us back by helicopter. The succulent salmon and lamb were served with great style. Sun was glinting onto the mullioned lead-glass Elizabethan windows, which looked out on the two hundred lush acres of gardens and woodland.

Later that day I found Gwyn, one of three gardeners, who was digging cheer-fully in the walled vegetable garden. The garden was filled with raspberries and currants for the restaurant's chef, although the patches of rhubarb had already been depleted for the kitchen. Yellow and red daylillies were intermixed with beds of zucchini and lettuce. We wandered from the vegetables, down a woodland path where the grass path was edged with white Queen Anne's lace and lavender loose-strife. The view over pastures to the Snowdonia Mountains filled the eye with softly outlined blue and gray ridges. Another path led back to the castle along a stream edged with green hostas in lavender and white bloom. Our own small three-story cottage, the Gingerbread House, overlooked the oldest garden on the place, a seven-teenth-century knot garden. The walled rectangular garden presented a colorful, controlled view. The box-edged circles, triangles, and domes were filled with laven-der rosemary buzzing with bees, alternating with yellow-flowered, gray-leaved santolina. The mix of lavender, gray, and yellow produced a colorful, painterly impact. There are more than nineteen cottages on the grounds and sixteen bedrooms within the castle itself. I ended each day with a walk to the spa to enjoy the steam bath, the hot tub, and the heated salt-water swimming pool. Given daytime temperatures in the low 60s, a warm and inviting swimming pool was indeed a luxury.

One day I hiked up to the obelisk, located in green pastures above Bodysgallen Hall. I found locals out walking with dogs and a couple riding two stylish gray horses. When I asked the way from Oliver, one of the doormen at Bodysgallen, he offered to take me to the starting point. In the dark of the oak trees, I asked if there were any bears. He responded, "Why, no, Madam, we have no bears; but Wales has many dragons!" Undeterred, I sallied forth to the top of the hill.

That afternoon, with blue skies and brilliant sun, we ventured the six miles to Bodnant garden. Bodnant is in the Conwy Valley with vistas of the mountains of Snowdonia. We entered near the half-timbered Victorian mansion whose nineteenth-century glass house was still filled with tender plants. Steps with balustrades lead down to a huge pond filled with pink water lilies. The intense sun turned the rosy colored lily pads silver. Borders filled with hydrangeas in white, lavender, deep purple, and blue lined the beds overlooking this fish-filled reflecting pond. We ambled down another flight of stairs and discovered the pin mill with its reflecting canal.

Sitting on the William Kent–styled bench, we observed a couple with a young son who delighted in catching frogs. He had found a frog walk consisting of five-inch-wide wooden steps for frogs to enter and exit the pond. The garden is known for its early spring plants, including azaleas, rhododendron, and camellias. We climbed down the dell along the Hiraethlyn River among enormous old conifers, red woods, and sequoias. It was rushing with white water, and the banks were thick with ferns and blue hydrangeas. We climbed back to the top and entered the famous tunnel of yellow laburnums. On our way out I met one of the many gardeners, Troy Scott Smith, who was busy creating a new garden by the entrance.

Next morning our destination was Powis Castle, built in the thirteenth century by the princes of Powys. This rosy rock fortress occupies a high hillock, with its garden terraces sloping to the southeast. The outlook from each of the mullioned windows is of green, sheep-filled pastures, toward the ancient, south-sloping, terraced gardens embedded in the hill. In the distance on the flat ground below is a fountain in the formal garden planned by the Fourth Marquis Herbert in the 1900s. The castle is frequented today by Charles, the Prince of Wales, and in earlier times by the Herberts and Lord Clive of East India fame. There was much to enjoy in the luxurious interior, but for me the central gallery with its Italian marble busts of twelve Caesars was special. There was also an Adam and Eve plaster work dating from 1593, and a one thousand-year-old Roman marble cat that the First Lord Clive brought back to Briton from his travels.

Outside the four Italianate terraces that descend the hillside beckon. Four hundred-year-old yews, dating from 1660, burnish the top slope, providing a sleek dark-green counterpoint to the colorful perennial borders. The borders were at their peak of July splendor with lavender clematis and pink sweet peas competing for room on the Victorian loops. A young gardener, Vicki Stelfox, was busy weeding the head-high pink and lavender fuchsia. She said that work began each morning at 8:00 and that 4:30 was quitting time. Another gardener, Edwin Hulzn, from the Netherlands, was deep in a border filled with blue and purple delphiniums, intermixed with yellow day lilies and pink roses. He advised that there was never sufficient time in the day to do all the pruning, weeding, and fertilizing to produce such an efflorescence of blooms. I especially loved the four lead statues of shepherds and shepherdesses, each with a small dog or lamb, adorning the second terrace with its glass-enclosed arboretum. Another focal point is a powerful Hercules battling a three-headed hydra snake. The Powis Castle and garden have the special charm of combining splendid flower gardens viewed against an expansive rural countryside. The blue and lavender of phlox and delphinium stand out against the blue and green of an enveloping vista. The yellow and green of daylilies and asters sparkle against a glinting sun.

Coming back to Bodysgallen after these adventures was like returning to a special country retreat. There were gatherings to celebrate birthdays and families enjoying a weekend. We were included in conversations, and many people were slightly startled that Charleston, South Carolina, was home. That evening around the fireside, we were seated next to a ninety-year-old father and his beautiful wife, who were accompanied by their son and daughter-in-law. They told us that driving on the left side of the road required the expertise of a fifty-year-old rather than a senior. The son was beaming with pride and delight at the vintage Jaguar he was driving.

Our last adventure at Bodysgallen was climbing to the top of the fifth-century tower. Oliver took us up the curving, narrow staircase. At the top were vistas in every direction of Conwy Castle, the sea, and the mountains of Snowdonia. Saying goodbye was a promise to return, or "à la prochaine fois."

If you go:
Bodnant Garden, south of Llandudno on the A470, open daily, 10 to 5

Powis Castle, south of Welshpool on the A483, open daily, except Monday,
12 noon to 4 P.M.

www.bodysgallen.co.uk; macj@bodysgallen.com

Part 6

Germany

FROM THE ISLAND OF RÜGEN TO
THE BAVARIAN MOUNTAINS

I learned to love Germany, its diverse landscape, and its welcoming people while living there in the spring of 1992. Our base was Bonn, which was still the capital of Germany and which was where my husband, Fred, was teaching law at Kaiser Wilhelm University. With bicycles and rail passes, we explored every corner of the country, from coastal towns such as Binz on the island of Rügen, to Berlin in the east and Munich in the south. One of my favorite gardens is Insel Mainau in the middle of Lake Constance. I was attracted to this spot because it is a seasonal garden, much like my own garden on Lake Summit in the mountains of western North Carolina. In the spring Insel Mainau features tulips, daffodils, peonies, and irises, while in fall it has thousands of dahlias. Dahlias were discovered in Central America and came to Europe through Spain in the 1780s. Today there are more than twenty thousand varieties, and the abundance and beauty of the dahlia are serenaded every fall on Insel Mainau. The chief gardener at Insel Mainau provided me his planting guide for creating a dahlia garden: plant after the last frost, with the plant tubers (their eyes or growing points) up, six inches deep in rich, well-drained soil in a sunny spot; water after plants are one-foot tall; nourish with a mix of well-rotted manure, compost, and 5.10.10 fertilizer; and dig up tubers after frost blackens the foliage, cut stems to a few inches, wash off soil, and place in a cardboard box covered with sawdust.

The following four essays explore a few of the many garden spots in Germany. This sampling barely scratches the surface. To find more German garden spots, look to Charles Quest-Ritson's *The Garden Lover's Guide to Germany*. ❧

Inspiration for a Fall Garden

Insel Mainau and Lake Constance

FALL IN NORTH CAROLINA IS APPLE-PICKING and dahlia season. My own garden comes to fruition with lavender, gold, red, and yellow dahlias of all sizes. Facing south, it is backed by a granite stone wall. In winter the southeast exposure to sun creates a microclimate so the bulbs come back season after season. I wanted more knowledge about the many varieties of dahlias and how best to cultivate these exotic flowers. A trip to Insel Mainau on the shores of Lake Constance in Germany provided that inspiration.

Insel Mainau is an island four miles from the ancient city of Constance. Grand Duke Friedrick I of Baden (1826–1907) purchased the 111-acre island in 1853 and began a garden in 1871. Our adventure began with the short fifty-mile trip from the Zurich airport to an appointment with the head gardener, Jürgen Koslich. The garden has more than two million visitors a year and a staff of eighty, and more than two hundred thousand Euros (or roughly three hundred thousand dollars) a year is spent on plants. With such a budget the meticulous care of every inch of ground is not surprising.

We drove across a small iron bridge, observing the thousands of ducks on the glinting water of Lake Constance. We parked below the orange and white Baroque palace where the descendants of the Grand Duke still live. Magnificent poplar trees and sequoias line the walk to the palace. Below the palace there is an Italian-style rose garden, and pink roses climb pergolas that edge the formal garden. We enjoyed the tranquil beauty of the rose garden framed by the deep blue vistas of Lake Constance.

A path leads to the top of a water cascade. From there we caught the first glimpse of the twelve thousand dahlias below. Jürgen explained that they purchase the dahlias as cuttings with roots from three different suppliers and plant the cuttings each year in April. The flowers in each bed have a uniform height. He ascribes this to using the cuttings rather than bulbs. The blooms are abundant, five feet high and profuse. We gazed over huge swathes whose color ranged from oranges to yellows, reds, whites, lavenders, and deep purples. The whole bedding scheme is framed on one side by yellow lindens and orange maples and on the other by Lake Constance. Winding paths frame routes for exploring this colorful maze.

We found a seat in the sun and listened to Jürgen's tips for the perfect dahlia bed: ample limed soil that is replaced every several years; new plants every year; meticulous watering; ample sun; and regular dead-heading of blooms. He expects the colorful display to last until frost. Each year Insel Mainau holds a Dahlia Queen event. Boxes along our route let us vote for the most perfect dahlia. With more than 215 varieties, visitors are faced with a bewildering array of choices: smooth, crinkled, showy, or subdued. At the butterfly house we had tea and apple pie while enjoying the amazing display of butterflies. Jürgen reminded us to come back in April and May, when a display of millions of daffodils and tulips brings springtime alive. The daffodils return each year as they have for the past forty years, spreading out over the hillsides. The tulips are replaced every two years to ensure maximum size and color. We left Insel Mainau with a replenished vision for our own fall garden.

Constance itself is a lovely old town. Our hotel, the Steigenberger Inselhotel, provides bicycles. We biked throughout the town enjoying the Friday market, the open shops, and the expectant air of Oktoberfest. There is music, drinking, and gatherings of friends. Our hotel had been an ancient monastery with an open courtyard. Murals depict life on Lake Constance, and our room had a balcony from which we could watch the sun set over the lake. The countryside of Bavaria is unspoiled, green, full of gray cows.

While waiting on a street corner in Constance for Fred, I struck up a conversation with a young architect who had bicycled all the way from Hamburg in two weeks. I was impressed at such an undertaking. He was powered by "green" inspiration, riding for charity to raise money to build water towers in Guatemala. Northern Germany is dotted by power-generating windmills. It is not surprising that a "green" movement is sustained in such a place. My newfound biking friend told me that it was possible to bike the entire way around Lake Constance. When I return to Lake Constance, my inspiration will be to take a biking tour to enjoy the beauty of the lake, the sweet smells of spring, and the intense high that comes from a bicycle adventure.

If you go:
(Tel. +49 (0) 75 31 303 138, Fax +49 (0) 75 31 303 160)
florian.heitzmann@mainau.de, www.mainau.de

www.steigenbergerinselhotel (Tel. 49 7531 125 0; Fax 49 7531 26402)

A Summer Visit to the Island of Rügen on the Baltic Sea

WHEN THE WEATHER IS HOT AND HUMID in Charleston, the question often arises as to where to go for a cool and refreshing visit. Many Charlestonians flock to Flat Rock, Saluda, Blowing Rock, Aspen, or Maine. If the goal is to practice a foreign language and take in a different culture, northern Germany, and especially the island of Rügen, should be considered.

A flight into Berlin brought us within easy reach of the Mecklenburg-Vorpommern region. Not long ago the entire region had been behind the Iron Curtain. The island of Rügen is dotted with fishing villages on the Baltic Sea. By 1880 it had become a European summer watering spot for the Belle Epoque era. The wonderful resort town of Binz is on the Ostsee, that is, the Baltic Sea. Our temporary home, now called the Grand Hotel Binz, is a preferred destination for fashionable Europeans. In the parking area before the hotel were two Lamborghinis whose proud owner was wearing not one but two diamond studs in his ears. The hotel is elegant with a spa swimming pool and two types of saunas.

With hotel bikes we set out to explore the town. Gingerbread-style balconies adorn summer houses that flank the boulevard along the sea. The town is in the German "Bader Architektur" style. Turreted roofs have fanciful wind vanes, and scalloped windows adorn houses. Pediments are burnished with swans, gargoyles, and other fanciful creatures, and iron scrollwork laces balconies. The new construction echoes the past, and the totality is splendid.

The crowning hour of the day was a hike through the towering beech forest along the high cliffs over the sea. The word *lapping* rightly describes the sound wafting up from the blue sea below. In places the sea is three hundred feet below the sheer white cliffs for which the Akona highland is famous. Within the woods we walked silently through deep leaves from many previous falls. The lower limbs have been trimmed by some unseen forester. Light filters through the green leaves and onto enormous gray trunks. Here and there we saw signs of some unknown lurking creature. At the highest point we stood facing the ocean with cool breezes blowing in our faces.

The beach is lined with *Strandkorbe* (bathing huts) for days when the wind might be blowing. This day the sun was hot and shining, and people were doing what is best done on beaches everywhere: building sand castles, sunning, playing ball in the water, and swimming. There were no waves, and the white sand was soft between our toes. There did not appear to be deep water unless one walked all the way to

Sweden. To my surprise a man disrobed right in front of me. I quickly turned my head only to discover that there were many naked men and women swimming and sunning.

The true reason to come to the island of Rügen is biking. In the high Alps of the Bernese Oberland, there are endless bikers, all of whom must eat nails for breakfast. Each longs to be a Lance Armstrong. The Alpine challenge is not found on the gentle hills of Rügen. In deep beech and fir forests, wonderful biking trails lead from one sea village to another. As I sailed downhill at top speed, I imagined that I was a youngster. What freedom! The trails are beautifully maintained and lead over hill and dale through managed forests.

Even though I speak German, it was very clear the minute I opened my mouth with a Charleston accent that I am not German. The Germans were totally puzzled as to my origin. They suspected Holland, but definitely not the United States. I asked one willing native why he thought I was a foreigner. He responded, "Why Frau, you do not have the melody." And I thought, "Heard melodies are sweet, but those unheard are sweeter."

A German breakfast is a treat to anticipate. Once, when I was a camper at Camp Green Cove in Tuxedo, I consumed eight doughnuts at one sitting. I was reminded of that as I ate eggs, bacon, potatoes, salmon, mushrooms, baked tomatoes, every type of bread, jam, yogurt, and endless cereals for breakfast on Rügen. No amount of biking, walking, and swimming could counteract this overindulgence.

There is a strange sensation while on vacation in a foreign land that time stands still. When we do not have routines to guide and direct us, time floats, seemingly endless. But, alas, the ultimate hour arrives, and it is time to go. In the words of Rudyard Kipling,

> "When earth's last picture is painted and the tubes are twisted and dried,
>   When the oldest colours have faded, and the youngest critic has died,
>   We shall rest, and, faith, we shall need it—lie down for an eon or two,
>   Til the Master of All Good Workmen shall put us to work anew!"

When the time to leave arrives, I hope to be sitting on a bluff high over the Baltic, watching the sun go down.

If you go: grandhotelbinz.com; www.ostsee.se/ruegers

Spring gardens at Insel Mainau on Lake Constance, Germany

The pool and garden at Linderhof, Ettal, Germany

The fountain at King Ludwig II's Linderhof, Ettal, Germany

The view of Linderhof from the Temple of Love, Ettal, Germany

Berlin

The Heart of the New Germany

I HAVE HAD THE GOOD LUCK TO WATCH BERLIN become one city and begin to shine. In the process it has been a city under intense construction with dug-up streets, monuments in various stages of rehabilitation, and shining new glass towers next to ugly, cheaply constructed structures of the Communist regime.

I first entered Berlin in the summer of 1992. My husband, Fred, was an exchange law professor from the University of Tennessee in Knoxville to Kaiser Wilhelm University in Bonn. Berliners whom we had met on the Blue Ridge Parkway in a view pullover had invited us to spend the weekend. The memory of the visit resonates with the sounds of an all-Beethoven symphony performance led by Claudio Abbado, a visit to Potsdam, and seeing San Souci, the home of Frederick the Great. Frederick had welcomed French Huguenots to Germany when they were being persecuted by Louis XIV, who had revoked the Edict of Nantes. Later, in 2001, we returned to Berlin to visit with the head of the Egyptian section of the museum and to enjoy the beautiful castle and garden of Charlottenburg, as well as to see the much-coveted Head of Nefertiti.

Back again in Berlin because of the Francisco Goya (1746–1828) exhibit at the National Gallery of Berlin, we stayed on the seventh floor of the Adlon, a Kempinski Hotel at the Brandenburg Gate. The view of the Reichstag, with its waving yellow, black, and orange flags was just out of our windows. The elegant hotel was filled with wealthy Germans. The sumptuous lobby was adorned with flowers, statues, and water fountains. Our room looked out over the "quadriga," the four horses that stand above the Brandenburg Gate.

The city seemed overwhelming. Everywhere there were vast buildings, huge spaces, large crowds, and too much cement. The weather was definitely cold for August 6. The high amid rain showers and wind was hardly 55 degrees. But we had come for a purpose, and so, with the wonderful assistance of the concierge at the Adlon Hotel, we procured a much desired ticket for the Goya exhibit.

Long lines circled the museum. I had known Goya from my art appreciation class at Sweetbriar only as the court painter of the aristocracy of Spain of the eighteenth century. He earned handsome commissions painting the royalty. With respect to all of his other paintings, he said, "I paint only what I want to paint." In a multitude of small drawings and paintings, he recorded the world he saw around him. I quickly realized that I was in for a modern-day horror show. I am too old and perhaps too wise to believe in witches, cannibals, demons, and other horrors that inhabit the nether world. But these were etched in vivid and wrenching ink and oil in Goya's small paintings and drawings. What anguish! What horror! Rarely has one man so strongly depicted the surreal dreams of nightmares. As Goya said, "I no longer fear witches, and goblins. All I fear are human beings." One painting is etched in my mind's eye. It was titled "The Dream of Reason," although it was a horrific nightmare. It may mean that we in our consciousness rely on reason, only to find that reason disintegrates and offers no palliative in an unhinged world. Goya's scenes of prisons, insane asylums, and the chaos of war suggest the repulsive degradation to which humanity can descend and his brushstrokes are foreshadowed and echoed by the monstrous events of later history.

Is this bleak view of humanity a prescient image for our time? Goya painted the inmates in the prisons, the insane in the asylum, the blind, the beggars, the madmen. And then he painted the dreams of cannibals, wild owls, witches, ghosts, goblins. There are scenes of personal horror such as babies gathered up in baskets by witches. Goya's nightmares reflected the Inquisition, as well as the destruction of Spain's wars with France.

Goya's images resonate today. If he had been present on 9/11, he would have painted the explosion of human bodies and the scattering of human remains. As Thomas Hobbes said, "and the life of man, solitary, poor, nasty, brutish, and short"—this is what Goya painted.

It amazed me that this Goya art show was enjoying such success in Berlin. However, the German people are not far removed from the destruction of World War II, its legacy of guilt feelings, and the brutal regime of the Communists in East Germany. It is often said that Germans feel an affinity for Southerners. Had I visited Charleston during or after the Civil War, it might have been far easier for me, like the Berliners of today, to conjure up the phantasmagoric images that were so evident in Goya's small drawings and paintings.

If you go: Hotel Adlon Kempinski Berlin, www.hotel-adlon.de

Germany

Schloss Linderhof, Ettal Cloister, and Oberammergau

FROM TIME TO TIME, I HAVE THE PLEASURE OF SEEING the humdrum parts of my life in a startling new light. Sometimes an old voice sounds like the first time I heard it, or the ten thousandth view from my back porch reveals a new bird's nest. So it is with travel. Going back in a different season to the same old place brings entirely new sights and feelings.

This past September, I was in Schloss Linderhof. Many years earlier, I had visited it in December after a snow. The gardens then were hidden under the drifts of white powder. An autumn return was a thrill. The air was intensely clear, the sky was azure blue, and the rugged mountains were sprinkled with a golden glow from beech, maples, and lindens.

Linderhof is a showcase house and garden. The house has four palatial rooms. Each interior room is closely linked to an exterior garden room. Built in 1870 by King Ludwig II, the last king of Bavaria, this stage set is a Rococo extravaganza. At the front portal Atlas is holding the night sky aloft. In front of the castle, the gilded goddess Flora is the centerpiece to a fountain that rises one hundred feet. Beyond Flora are terraced gardens up the hillside to a focal point: a Corinthian temple with a marble Venus.

The back portal looks from Ludwig's gilt and blue bedroom to a cascade with Neptune on four horses. Neptune's Tritons are blowing bugles that gush water. At the top of the water staircase is a reflecting water parterre and a green gazebo, known as the music pavilion. Ludwig's dining room, glowing in gilt and red, has a table set for one; the table emerges from the kitchen below on a pulley system. The solitary diner looks out on the east garden, where a statue of Fame blows a gilded trumpet.

Welcoming Germans who were enjoying the sun seemed delighted to speak with us, the only Americans present. One asked, wryly, if we were fleeing a hurricane. We walked the extensive grounds and found Ludwig's surprise follies—a hunting lodge built around a huge ash tree echoed Richard Wagner's "Hundinghutte" from the music-drama *Die Walküre*. The gold-leaf dome of a Moorish kiosk glints in the sunlight. Its interior is decorated with a ceramic peacock throne. However, the most astounding folly is the Venus Grotto, built of vaulted steel clad with red brick and covered with a sand and cement finish to simulate the interior of a natural grotto. Here Ludwig seated himself in a gilded boat in the form of a mussel shell and witnessed performances of Richard Wagner's operas. Ludwig had delusions of grandeur. He longed to be Louis XIV, and Linderhof is full of portraits and statues of the French royalty. He lived a solitary life full of fantasy. He died mysteriously in 1886, when he was only forty-five years of age. Linderhof epitomizes his search for beauty which would delight later generations of tourists from throughout the world.

We left Linderhof for Ettal, a mile away. Ettal Cloister is a Benedictine monastery. Set in a narrow mountain valley, its imposing three domes tower over a white exterior. The interior blooms with gilt, pink and white marble, dramatic altars, and frescoes from the life of Jesus. Today the cloister is a school for more than five hundred children from neighboring towns and is also a vital parish church. I asked a group of young girls what subjects they were studying and was impressed by the answer—English, French, Latin, and Greek! They were soon off to catch the bus to Oberammergau, also our destination for the night.

Oberammergau is in the Ammertal, the valley of the Ammer River. It is a green valley, sloping up to fir-covered mountains. The gently sloping valley has wonderful western exposure and long daylight hours. The town is known for the Passion Play and for its many wood-carvers. These talented artisans produce smiling fairy-tale figures, laughing clowns, majestic eagles, and other handcrafted woodwork. We located a craftsman, Paul Fraserei, who showed us through his workshop, which was full of wood dust, machines, and half-finished images. Two shop owners had especially beautiful wood carvings: Florian Lang at 20 Dorfstrasse had a magnificent eagle carved by Jürgen Kirchner, and Anton Baur at 27 Dorfstrasse had exquisite mirrors modeled after Gustav Klimt. We stayed in the Parkhotel Sonnenhof, which has a welcoming heated swimming pool. We watched the sun set from a cozy balcony under the eaves.

The memory of Linderhof, Ettal, and Oberammergau is still fresh. How would it look in springtime when the flower beds are freshly planted with tulips and daffodils? Will the sound of crickets be replaced by the song of a wren? With luck I may see this splendid place in still another season.

If you go:
Parkhotel Sonnenhof, Oberammergau. www.parkhotel-sonnenhof.de

Schloss Linderhof (Tel. 08822 920311)

Part 7

Iberia

THE MOORISH INFLUENCE

The gardens of southern Spain reflect their Moorish influence, aridity, and the imaginative use of water. The gardens of the island of Madeira evoke its year-round temperate climate and its remoteness in the Atlantic Ocean from the Iberian peninsula and the African continent. The gardens of southern Portugal share the successes of the gardens of the Southern Spain, France, and Italy which have overcome the difficult problems of aridity and occasionally strong sea breezes.

Water is a key element in these gardens. It is used for ornamentation and for its life-giving qualities that were so essential in these early communities. In the Alhambra, featured in the first essay, water is abundant in fountains and quiet pools. It reflects the exquisite buildings and the sky in all its daytime and evening beauty. Water is also there for its splashing and tinkling sounds. The garden of Alfabia on Majorca abounds in a rich and diverse use of water. Another common factor in many of the featured gardens is the unique topography. The islands are mountainous, with hillside gardens predominating in Majorca and in Madeira.

In Spanish and Portuguese gardens there is great emphasis on the use of shrubs and flowers to create separate and private enclosures. Madeira has a climate that permits trees and shrubs from faraway temperate places such as South America and New Zealand to flourish. Quinta do Palheiro, a garden on Madeira, has small topiary, as well as a fine array of tree ferns, camellias, and rhododendrons. One of my favorite Madeira gardens is the Jardim Botanico da Madeira, with its stunning color schemes and amazing vista of the Atlantic Ocean over the city of Funchal. We based at Reid's Palace Hotel. There we enjoyed its fruitful and orchid-filled garden, which provided the perfect setting for discovering the plants and flowers of this exotic island. ❧

Christmas in Majorca

EAST WIND, GRAY SKIES, AND CHILLY DECEMBER DAYS in Charleston make me long for an adventure in the sun. The island of Majorca, a part of Spain in the middle of the Mediterranean Sea, has held a fascination for me since reading George Sand's *A Winter in Majorca.* The island is bucolic, filled with groves of orange and lemon trees. In February the island becomes a white cloud of flowering almonds. As George Sand described, "the Island is a veritable painter's Eldorado . . . , a green Switzer-land, beneath a Calabrian sky, with a silence and solemnity of the Orient. . . . Rocky peaks stand silhouetted against a sparkling sky." Sand had spent the winter of 1838 on the island with Frédéric Chopin. Their home was the vintage monastery Real Cartuja de Valldemossa.

Our home in Majorca was La Residencia, an Orient Express Hotel in the charming east-coast town of Deia. La Residencia is like a small village, full of low-key activities and friendly residents. Built on nine levels at the top of a rocky hillside, the highest level contains a fully equipped gym and spa. Lower levels have indoor and outdoor swimming pools. The hotel is located in two vintage Spanish estate buildings that have been beautifully restored. Breakfast is served in their fabulous restaurant, El Olivo.

Inside, fireplaces burn brightly with olive wood. There are beautiful Christmas decorations on each mantel. Comfortable sofas and chairs invite guests to relax and enjoy the special ambience. Outside, tennis courts buzz with action, presided over by the club's tennis pro, Shayne Tabb. There are afternoons of mixed doubles. Other afternoons are devoted to cooking classes with the chef, who teaches us the art of making chocolate pudding. Easy friendships develop, so that convivial groups dine together each evening in the many fine restaurants of Deia.

The town is an artist colony with many resident painters, and we enjoyed vis-iting their studios. At David Templeton's studio each painting presents a paradox. One lady with lacy underwear is either stepping in or out of her pants, depending on whether the painting is presented up or down. At Authuro's studio there is a superb copy of a Vermeer-like lady whose sunglasses reflect the tulip-filled fields of Holland. We were also amused by an entrancing mermaid who looked longingly at a pair of pointed high heels.

Our days were spent in excursions to gardens and small towns only a short dis-tance from Deia. The drive along the coastal route provided spectacular views of the ocean and mountains.

Vista from Son Morroig, near Deia, Majorca

The Moors controlled Majorca for centuries, where they developed irrigation channels to preserve water during the dry season. Their unique garden style was evident in Alfabia, a lovely water-filled garden. Five centuries ago it had been a lush Moorish estate. Now long walks are covered with pergolas festooned with wisteria, bougainvillea, honeysuckle, and jasmine. There are ivy-covered walls and water channels. On one walk we pressed a button, and jets of water arched up over the path. Bamboo, palms, and bulrushes create a jungle effect, and the garden is surrounded by orange and lemon groves. We were amused by a herd of goats with baby goats who jumped about bleating, while fat black pigs grunted and snorted.

Son Morroig is an Italian-style villa that occupies a stunning promontory over-looking the Mediterranean. On our visit we found the grizzled old caretaker and his dog sitting before a warm fire. Archduke Ludwig Salvator of Austria (1847–1915), who had been born in the Pitti Palace in Florence, built this superb palace. Memories of home haunted his dreams. He created a neoclassical temple of Carrara marble on a promontory overlooking the sea. We stood in the gloaming under the temple and watched the opalescent sea change from blue to green and pink as the sun set.

In the nineteenth and previous centuries all work had required intense physical labor of men and women. La Granga focused on the traditional arts and how such work used to be done, which was fascinating. We learned how wine and olive oil were made, how hemp was dyed, and how people performed the multifarious tasks of a farm. We stopped at the open kitchen, sampling wine and Christmas bread made of figs and almonds. The house dates from 1239 and was the foundation of the Cistercian Order in Majorca. Today it is a privately owned museum with traditional arts. From the loggia a vast estate spreads out toward the towering, blue mountains. A rushing river plummets down through tall plane trees.

The island of Majorca is rural, unspoiled, and warm year round. Away from the hub of Palma, it is a country of small farms, green valleys, plains, and, on the northern edge, towering snowcapped mountains. It is also a country of coves and beaches. The winding coast road leads from Deia, our home base, to Soller, a port on the northern coast. We hiked up to the lighthouse at Soller to enjoy a panoramic

Water jets in the garden at Alfabia, Majorca

view of the harbor. The Soller Botanic Garden is set on a hillside with terraced plots containing collections of the island's indigenous flora. We wandered through it enjoying the birdsong and smell of aromatic herbs.

My final memory of Majorca is of wandering through the monks' cells and gardens at the Real Cartuja at Valldemossa. George Sand and Frédéric Chopin stayed here, and memories of them still linger. Sand saw Majorca as a paradise, rather like Rousseau's state of nature. From her small monastery garden the island reflects this sublime state. We left Majorca reluctantly, hoping that another Christmas season would bring us back.

If you go:
www.hotellaresidencia.com

www.arturorhodes.com

davidtem@gmail.com

Barbara Segall, *The Garden Lover's Guide to Spain and Portugal*

The Spanish Costa del Sol

Marbella Club Hotel and a Side Trip to Granada

WE ARRIVED AT THE MALAGA TRAIN STATION from Madrid on a fast Talgo train called Ave. The train pummeled through the black night, while the twinkling lights of homes disappeared instantly. We found our rental car and were off in the fresh night air for the Marbella Club Hotel on the Spanish Costa del Sol, an oasis by the sea.

The soothing sounds of water are everywhere at Marbella Club on the Spanish Costa del Sol. The club is set in a renowned garden. Fountains of every shape and size create dramatic water focal points in the garden. A white marble fountain tinkles. An "everyman" column under the gazebo oozes, and the wall of water behind the salt water pool gurgles. In the distance the roar of the gray-green ocean pounds. White-capped waves foam inward to sprawl along the shore line. The sky is blue overhead with a strong east wind whipping the Marbella Club flags.

Water is life to a garden, and it is available here in abundance. My guide to the club garden was Javier Viaido. He had studied horticulture and landscape arts at the University at Barcelona. Best of all his English flowed easily as we walked and talked among the courtyards and pergola-covered walks. The fruit of a December orchard was abundant with orange, lemon, and lime trees. Each tree is skillfully pruned to provide see-through transparency toward other points of interest. The fronds of coconut and Canary Island palms waved gently overhead. Their old fronds had been lanced, giving them a manicured appearance. We explored the gardens on tile walks, covered with pergolas of yellow euphorbia. Bougainvillea in shades of orange, lavender, and purple hang from balconies, and the juxtaposition of purple and orange colors creates a lively rainbow effect against the deep green of the many subtropical plants. There are banana trees, jacaranda trees, and a funny tree covered with sharp spikes that Javier said the locals called a "drunk stick." Any drunk who happened to lean against such a tree would certainly get a dreadful spanking.

The wind swirled through the garden, making olive branches loaded with their green and black fruit dance up and down. I learned that green olives can be picked, soaked in lemon and salt water, and added to salads. The black ones were ready for picking for the olive oil harvest. The sago palms were full of breadlike fruit that can be made into pungent bread. The horn-shaped datura in yellow and pink were bobbing like bells overhead. My favorite part of the garden is an enclosed courtyard with four huge ficus trees that are underplanted for the Christmas season with crimson cyclamen and poinsettias. The garden is alive with birdsong and the mewing

Reflecting pool, the Alhambra, Granada, Spain

of gulls overhead. Javier left me with a one-world story. He had courted a young lady from Auburn, Alabama who had come to Spain to practice her Spanish. When I asked her name he smiled, "Jennifer Hunt," and then "Oh, no, Jennifer Lee Hunt: every Southern lady must have a middle name!"

Our next destination was Granada and the Alhambra. We arrived at the Parador of Granada, the Hotel San Francisco, which has style and Old World elegance. It was here that Isabella and Fernando were originally buried, after their spectacular siege and conquest of Granada in 1492. This victory provided new resources to send Christopher Columbus on his voyages to "China." The Parador is located in the middle of the Alhambra, making it the perfect spot for enjoying the splendid walks, gardens, and buildings of the Alhambra.

The Citadel of the Alhambra encompasses many centuries, many cultures, and several palaces. The Casas Reales is the Moorish palace complex of the Nasrid dynasty, the last Islamic dynasty to rule in Spain. Of special delight for me was the highest point, the Generalife, where we are closest to paradise. Here the play of water and the fountains across the long narrow pools gives a feeling of enormous sensuality and peace. From this high point the vista encompasses the entire Citadel of the Alhambra. The drama of history and the intensity of light makes the Alhambra special.

I left Spain with a determination to learn the Spanish language, an important skill in a country where English is rarely heard.

If you go:
reserves@marbellaclub.com

www.parador.es

Hotel San Francisco, Parador Granada

Barbara Segall's *The Garden Lover's Guide to Spain and Portugal*

Water jets, in the Generalife garden at the Alhambra, Spain

Traveling to Madeira

ONE BLUSTERY GRAY DAY IN MARCH WE SET OFF for Lisbon and Madeira. We were traveling in the footsteps of my great-grand aunt, Elizabeth "Lizzie" Sinkler Coxe. Her trip had begun in February of 1902, on a slow steamer from New York City, with a brief layover in Madeira for refueling. Lizzie arrived in the port of Funchal and made her way by ox-drawn sledge to the English Hotel on the hill overlooking the harbor. She described it as having every modern convenience, including a lift, electric lights, hygienic facilities throughout, an English chapel, and an English doctor. Many years later Sir Winston Churchill came to the English Hotel, now called Reid's Palace, and painted seascapes *en plein aire.*

We arrived at the same hotel by car, and a century later it still has every modern convenience including a business center for e-mail, two heated swimming pools (one with sweet water and one with salt), a spa center for massages and workout, and several elegant restaurants. The garden was filled with the bounty of a tropical climate. The frangipani flower trees were just coming into bloom, and the delicate lavender blooms of the jacaranda were bouncing against a strong breeze. There were coral blooms on the African tulip tree, and orange and cerise flowers on the bougainvillea. Sprinkled around this exotic scene were huge old camellias covered with pink and rose blossoms, and azaleas pruned to look like elegant trees covered with lavender flowers. The weather was perfect with a high of 65 and a low of 57.

Lizzie was enthralled with the exotic beauty of Madeira. As she said, "All afternoon we were passing close to beautiful islands, which are mountains rising out of the sea, and all up the steep sides were sparkling waterfalls and cascades of pink and red bougainvilleas and chalets. . . . The moon hung overhead and the lights twinkled under the avenue of great sycamore trees where many attractive booths of baskets and embroideries and picturesque cages of parrots hung. . . . As we drove up to the English Hotel on the heights, we could see in the moonlight through great gateways, gardens with hedges of calla lilies, walls covered with heliotrope that scented the night air" (Elizabeth Sinkler Coxe, *Tales from the Grand Tour, 1890–1910,* edited by Anne Sinkler Whaley LeClercq, p. 85).

Lizzie was picked up by a canvas hammock carried by two persons, and she spent the day enjoying the sights and sounds of a busy island. She marveled that every woman was busy with embroidery while there were no visible signs of the island's famed Madeira wine being sold or distilled. Lizzie was taken in her fashionable hammock up the steep switchbacks to Monte, high above the port city of

Funchal. There she witnessed toboggans, or wooden sleds, each being run down the steep slopes by a jaunty two-person team of locals.

We too went to Monte, but, instead of taking the sleigh ride, we visited the tropical garden, Monte Palace. Monte Palace is a luxury hotel that has been restored as a garden by a local wine merchant. The garden covers seventeen acres of undulating landscape filled with cycads from South Africa. There are vibrant collections of azaleas, heathers, orchids, proteas, and tree ferns. Throughout the garden one can find blue and turquoise tiles from Madeira intermingled with Japanese icons brought from Japan in the seventeenth century. The garden is full of the sound of rushing water and the cry of peacocks whose dazzling tails flash blue and green in the sunlight.

We left Monte for Camacha to enjoy the inviting garden of Quinta do Palheiro Ferreiro. Also known as Blandy's Garden, after the English family that has owned it since 1884, it is a three-tiered English-style garden. A flight of steps leads down to a sunken garden with an octagonal pool and clipped boxwood topiary in the shape of birds. On the other side of the sunken garden is an area called the inferno with a small steep valley holding tree ferns, camellias, and rhododendron. The

Men of Madeira and their sleigh-riding customers, Funchal, Madeira

whole garden covers thirty acres. We settled in at a small teahouse to enjoy the buzz of bees and the sparkling cool day.

We returned to our balcony at Reid's Palace, overlooking a pink and opal sea. The ever-present sea on the island of Madeira is at times azure-tinged with green and at other times a gray flecked with lavender and purple. Clouds of fluffy white and gray float overhead. Pigeons plummet from the cliffs into the brink and then circle back to the top, while gulls ride the crest of waves. Christopher Columbus (1451–1506) made his home in one of the Madeira Islands, Porto Santo. One respects mastery of the sea lanes by Columbus, Vasco da Gama (c. 1469–1524), and Pedro Alvares Cabral (1467–1520). They lived by the sea and were fearless explorers. Vasco da Gama rounded Africa and the Cape of Good Hope in 1498 to establish Portuguese colonies in India and China. Cabral, leading a fleet of thirteen ships, made his way in 1500 to what is now called Brazil and then sailed to India to trade for valuable spices.

The drinking hour beckoned as did the stylish Cipriani restaurant. The restaurant hangs over a cliff looking to the western sky. We began with a pungent quail salad. The delicious little birds were hidden in a bed of tartly seasoned greens. That treat was followed by filet of sole in a browned butter sauce with lemon, *au meuniere.* Finally, a desert of vanilla ice cream topped with raspberry and Madeira wine sauce brought a delicious dinner to a wonderful conclusion.

Lizzie left Madeira on a "Cook's Steamer" for Gibraltar, then Naples, and finally Alexandria. She was a patient traveler, enjoying the long days by reading poetry or prose, embroidering, or sitting on one of Cook's Nile steamers and watching the lavender Libyan hills in the distance. She was a lady who loved beauty, thrilled to the company of her family, and looked forward to letters from home. Like Lizzie, I too waited for the mail, but it was the delightfully swift e-mail that brings word of the doings of family and friends. How different the world is today, and yet how the eternal verities of family, friends, and the beauty of nature still inspire and delight.

If you go:
Reid's Palace, Funchal, Madeira, is an Orient Express Hotel (Tel. 800 237 1236)

Quinta do Palheiro Ferreiro is five miles from Funchal on the EN 102 to Camacha

Jardim Tropical da Quinta do Monte Palace is located three miles north of Funchal in Monte. Each garden can be reached by either a private car or by taxi.

There are other wonderful gardens, and they can be found in *The Garden Lover's Guide to Spain and Portugal.* Lizzie's trip can be enjoyed in *Tales from the Grand Tour, 1890–1910,* which I edited from her own first-person accounts.

Part 8

Discovering Garden Spots Closer to Home

My mother, Emily Whaley, used to say that Charleston in June was like a spring bride all decked out in her best finery. Indeed Charleston is in bloom every season of the year. May, June, and July dazzle with pink and white oleander and pink, lavender, and white crepe myrtle. The city is lush and green. If you are lucky, in July an east wind will be blowing, cooling the atmosphere. Those sea breezes keep Charleston unexpectedly cool. My favorite garden season in Charleston is fall leaning into winter. The camellias begin to bloom in October. Their pink, lavender, and magenta hues abound in every city garden. By February camellias are at their peak. Most visitors know Charleston for its spring blooms. Historic Charleston Foundation puts on its House and Garden Tours from mid-March to the end of April, and the Preservation Society of Charleston hosts a delightful garden tour in the fall. Charleston also has many house museums with open gardens, such as the Nathaniel Russell House and the Heyward-Washington House. The gardens of both of those fine houses are always in bloom. Charleston's undiscovered gem is the garden at Hampton Park. It is lush with azaleas and camellias in winter and early spring. Its beds of perennials and roses are stunning in summer. The old bandstand dates from the Exposition.

Surrounding Charleston are the lovely and verdant swamps and rice fields of the South Carolina lowcountry. One of my favorite destinations among our barrier islands is Kiawah Island. Its paved bicycle paths lead through swamps and fields along lagoons filled with blue herons and white egrets. On a recent visit to Kiawah, the screaming sounds of an east wind enveloped me as I walked along the brilliant white sand beach.

The garden at the Sanctuary Hotel is a masterful seaside garden that perches on the shores of the Atlantic Ocean. My guide to this colorful, bird- and butterfly-filled garden was the outstanding horticulturist Peter Nelson. Peter is a plant man. He knows which species will flourish under the adverse conditions of wind, salt spray, and sun. He has used palms of every type to provide the structure for the Sanctuary's many garden spaces. He pointed to the pindo palm, often called a "jelly" palm as its fruit is used to make jelly in late summer. Other palms used at the Sanctuary include the dwarf cabbage palms and our state tree, the palmetto. Sago palms, with colorful red seeds, line brick walkways. Peter told me that he had handled an outbreak of scale with dormant oil spray which must be used when the temperature is less than 60 degrees.

Hollywood junipers provide focal points, while blue Pacific junipers provide ground cover. Both plants tolerate salt spray and wind. Old favorites, oleanders, wax myrtles, and viburnum, also shade walkways. Caressa hollies and Chinese hollies, loaded with bright red berries, surround the butterfly garden. Red-flowered bottle brush and buddleia have been planted in profusion to attract the orange butterflies of fall and the ruby-throated hummingbirds of summer. Peter pointed to the intrusion of deer that have dined on his Swiss chard, informing me that they are deterred by a deer spray called Liquid Fence.

The Sanctuary Hotel preserves a wildlife habitat including grasses and native shrubs, in hope of attracting bobcats, blue herons, egrets, ducks, and more of the wonderful world of nature that abounds on Kiawah Island. The Sanctuary is only thirty minutes from downtown Charleston. It is a wonderful destination for gardeners and vacationers, as well as being a place to savor the charms of the South Carolina lowcountry.

The following nine essays will transport you to garden spots in North Carolina, Florida, the Hudson River Valley, Boston, Philadelphia, and New Orleans. ❧

If you go: www.kiawahresort.com/accommodations/the-sanctuary

Biltmore, North Carolina

An Estate for All Seasons

MANY CITY DWELLERS NEVER FULLY THRILL to the excitement of the change of seasons. The Biltmore Estate is an enclave where each season comes and goes slowly and immerses you in the rhythmic cycles of nature. August is the height of the summer season, with roses brilliantly blooming in the formal garden in pink, white, red, and other vibrant colors. September offers a sweet transition to fall. November flames out with orange and red Japanese maples dotting the paths of the shrub garden. Spring arrives in May, with colorful displays of azaleas, rhododendron, and carpets of bulbs. Each month and season bring kaleidoscopic changes in the variety of blooming plants and the color of their foliage, but the castle itself is always there, ready to welcome and please Biltmore's many visitors. The estate vistas change dramatically according to time of day, weather, and the angle of declination of the sun. The morning mists often hang heavily over the valleys, leaving only the outlines of the mountain ridges apparent. The rose-colored sky of the setting sun creates altogether different, but pleasing impressions.

George W. Vanderbilt (1862–1914) was the grandson of the "Commodore," Cornelius Vanderbilt (1794–1877), one of the richest men in America. Having inherited part of the Vanderbilt fortune, he decided in 1888, at the age of twenty-five, to build a French-style chateau in the style of Blois, Chenonceau, and Chambord near Asheville. He called his estate Biltmore from "Bilt," the Dutch town from which his ancestors came, and "more" (or moor), an old English word for open, rolling land. Vanderbilt retained one of America's great architects, Richard Morris Hunt (1828–1895), and they traveled together in the Loire Valley of France to seek inspiration. Hunt was a society architect and the first American to study at the prestigious École de Beaux-Arts in Paris. He had designed Marble House and the Breakers in Newport, Rhode Island, as well as the facade of the Metropolitan Museum of Art in New York. Hunt's four-story, 175,000–square-foot mansion of Indiana limestone, completed in 1895, took seven years to build. The 250–room chateau featured the modern conveniences of steam heat, electricity, 33 family and guest bedrooms, 65 fireplaces, elevators, three kitchens, an indoor swimming pool, and 43 bathrooms. The original wood model of the chateau, with its cantilevered staircase, can be seen today. Vanderbilt purchased more than 125,000 acres of mountain land for Biltmore, and his property extended from the west terraces of the Biltmore castle more than 18 miles to and beyond Mount Pisgah. The unspoiled view-shed of the present 8,000-acre Biltmore Estate will be preserved as wilderness in perpetuity because most of Vanderbilt's vast acreage was conveyed to the United States to establish the Pisgah National Forest.

Vanderbilt retained Frederick Law Olmsted (1822–1903), America's greatest landscape gardener, who sought to evoke "the overwhelming sense of the bounteousness and mystery of nature that he had experienced in the tropics." Olmsted wanted to create "an aspect more nearly of sub-tropical luxuriance, than would occur spontaneously at Biltmore." Olmsted had been commissioned to design Central Park in New York City and the U.S. Capitol grounds in Washington. Vanderbilt was astute enough to heed Olmsted's advice: "Plan a small park as a foreground for the distant view, build some gardens close to the house, and devote the rest of his acres to forestry." Charles E. Beveridge and Paul Rocheleau, *Frederick Law Olmsted: Designing the American Landscape,* p. 194 (Universe Publishing, 1998). (The quoted materials in this essay are taken from Beveridge and Rocheleau's chapter eleven on the Biltmore Estate).

Olmsted suggested that ten thousand or more native rhododendron should be planted along the three-mile approach road to the castle and mixed with appropriate plants from across the world to "achieve the effect of richness, delicacy, and mystery." Olmsted searched for plants that would provide a variety of color and texture, plants that "increased the effect of complexity of light and shadow near the eye that was an essential element of his picturesque style." He wanted to create an illusion of extended space along the approach and other roads on the estate. He wanted "low growing, lustrous and fine flowering plants" in the center of the valley and "dense towering walls of foliage" on the steep side slopes. He envisioned "glints of sun-lighted bits of water with enough low foliage to make it intricate and mysterious, and to exclude the idea of there being anything artificial in what is seen." Biltmore's horticultural director, Parker Andes, said that his grounds crews in early fall must hoist scores of immense pots of sensitive tropical plants from their permanent clay or plastic containers to winter in the conservatory, and he replaces them with hardy evergreens for the Christmas season.

A ramble around the estate proves Olmsted's wisdom. Carriage roads are edged with mowed grass, while meadows dotted with large oak and poplar trees preserve the vistas to the blue ridges of the mountains. Fields of silage corn and soybeans for the estate's herd of black Angus cattle flourish along miles of the French Broad River. The ponds adjacent to the glistening rapids of the French Broad were constructed at the direction of Olmsted to enhance the water vista from the castle, and the ponds provide a haven for hundreds of geese and ducks. Visitors ride bicycles and horses along the riverbanks, and kayak rides on the French Broad River add to the excitement of outdoor adventures. There are Biltmore vineyards and a winery that welcomes visitors with free samples of the local Chablis and Merlot.

The Biltmore Mansion from the garden, Ashville, North Carolina

A tour of the gardens with Parker Andes provided a few clues to the intensity of the gardening endeavor. More than 108,000 spring blooming bulbs are planted in the formal walled garden every year. Each hole contains up to nine bulbs of two different varieties to extend the bloom season. In summer the formal garden is mass-planted with annuals, outlined with a brilliant mixture of red and green coleus, and in September there is a display of red and yellow chrysanthemums. The original conservatory of about 7,500 square feet still stands at the foot of the formal walled garden and is filled with orchids and other tropical plants. The Italian garden features three water parterres planted with lotus, yellow-blooming water cannas, red-stemmed thalia, maroon-leaved rice, blue, pink, and lavender water lilies, and gigantic Amazonica water lilies.

At Biltmore you can drive thirty miles of paved country roads through a pristine wilderness. So little in our land remains as it once was. But Biltmore remains, largely true to Olmsted's original vision: "The Estate . . . shall have throughout a natural and comparatively wild and secluded character; its borders rich with varied forms of vegetation . . . springs and streams and pools, steep banks and rocks, all consistent with the sensation of passing through the remote depths of a natural forest."

Biltmore today is an enormous enterprise with more than eighteen hundred employees. One of the star attractions is the inn, a luxurious destination, with a

The walled garden through an oval in the pergola, Biltmore Estate, Ashville, North Carolina

heated outdoor pool, Jacuzzi, and a spa. The ground-floor lounge is large and comfortable and resonates with the soft touches of the pianist in the bar area. The restaurant is first rate, and you get the vista of the Pisgah Range from the dining area. Staying on site at the inn for several days provides a glimpse of life from sunrise to moonrise in the valley of the French Broad River. We drove the grounds at dusk with the top down, enjoying the bleating of newborn lambs and the sighting of elusive deer. Cicadas' song told of shortened days and cooler nights, an antidote to the hot summer of 2010.

Biltmore was the last great project undertaken by Olmsted, and it consumed the last seven years of his professional life. Olmsted had spent most of his professional life on public projects. Prophetically, however, Olmsted realized that his efforts at Biltmore were "a private work of very rare public interest." Thus it would come as no surprise to him that Biltmore, though still privately owned and administered, should attract and offer inspiration, pleasure, and serenity to literally hundreds of thousands of guests each year, without seeming crowded at all because of the vast scale of the project that Olmsted prevailed on Vanderbilt to undertake.

If you go:
www.biltmore.com; www.biltmore.com/stay/

groupsales@biltmore.com

Tel. 828-225-6260

The Orchard Inn

A Mountain Destination in Saluda, North Carolina

THE ORCHARD INN IN SALUDA, NORTH CAROLINA, is a fine destination in spring, summer, or fall. Returning to the Orchard Inn is like a homecoming. It is always packed with friends, or friends of friends, from all over the South. Guests gather in the fall on comfortable sofas before the welcoming and roaring fire. The atmosphere is like a house party for adults. In spring friends gather on the porch to jog on the joggling board, and there is laughter and conviviality. The view of the mountains from the porch is framed by huge, old poplar trees. Lavender and white lilacs are abundant, and their aroma perfumes the air. The Orchard Inn complex includes the main inn and seven cabins or cottages, two of which are new. The inn was originally built in 1926 as a retreat for workers of the Southern Railway. The large, rambling house has a wonderful front porch, with bedrooms on the first and second levels. The rooms are comfortable with easy chairs, Goldilocks's "just right" beds, and deep tubs in the bathrooms.

The food at the Orchard Inn is a special treat. The setting on the enclosed back porch looks toward the South Carolina mountains. Six bird feeders are close by where cardinals, finches, titmice, and yellow orioles graze to their bellies' delight on specialty seeds, and for the rest of us, breakfast is a two-course gourmet feast included in the room rate. There are many small adventures, such as a day of hiking down to Pearson's Falls or biking down the Greenville watershed to Tryon. After a day of touring the Biltmore gardens or shopping at the Biltmore Village, returning to the Orchard Inn is a welcome retreat. Dinner is a masterpiece of crab cakes or filets. Jackets are encouraged for gentlemen. The four-course experience begins with a delicate soup, followed by a succulent salad. There are always two choices for the main course. My favorites are Pawley's Island crab cakes and tenderloin cooked to perfection.

Saluda is only a three-hour drive from Charleston. It has a host of lowcountry summer dwellers. Visitors know it for Coon Dog Day, when more than ten thousand folks gather to enjoy the scene. Most weekends it is a much quieter place, with diners going to the Purple Onion and shoppers enjoying the Brass Latch. On Sunday the old Episcopal church welcomes visitors. Garden lovers visit Walter Hoover's magic garden next to the Episcopal church on Charles Street. Hoover has gone into the business of selling rare Japanese irises, but his collection includes more than seventy varieties and all colors from white to pink to lavender. The three-petal beauties bloom from the first week of May through the first week of July.

Back at the Orchard Inn, old friends are embracing, and new friends are sitting in comfortable sofas or swinging under the pergola, watching the sun and shadows over the blue-green mountains. When the sun sets and "Taps" sounds, one of my favorite mountain venues is Saluda's Orchard Inn.

If you go: www.orchardinn.com; innkeeper@orchardinn.com (Tel. 800-581-3800 or 828-749-5471). Several private cottages are also available, and you may book a wedding reception as well.

Beyond Miami

Coral Gables, Vizcaya, and the Biltmore Hotel

BEYOND THE CULTURAL HODGEPODGE OF MIAMI, there is a green oasis that George Merrick (1862–1942) created in the 1920s. His family's house was made of coral and was capped with gables, hence the name of the town he founded, Coral Gables. Merrick envisioned a new Spain, giving streets names such as Granada, Toledo, and Sevilla. Two venerable sites loom large in the early history of the Miami area and are once again vibrant: the Biltmore Hotel in Coral Gables and Vizcaya Villa and Garden in Miami.

The Biltmore Hotel sits in the midst of two lush golf courses, the Biltmore and the Riviera. We enjoyed the ambience of the hotel and its golfing environs during the International Orange Bowl Junior Golf Championship. Seventeen-year-olds from around the world were showing off their scratch games, while adoring parents admired and encouraged. In the evenings we walked the green paths and crossed the Venetian-style bridges over lagoons. Parrots cackled overhead searching for a roost, while ducks quacked and hissed as we invaded their range. Lush fan palms and tall royal palms danced and waved in a gentle breeze. The heavens twinkled with stars against the purple and orange glow of twilight. We toasted the end of the year and marveled at 78 degrees during a December evening.

Earlier in the day we had relaxed in the sun around an enormous elbow-shaped swimming pool. The Biltmore's famous swimming instructor at one time was the Olympian Johnny Weismuller, known for his role as Tarzan. A gaggle of sun worshippers were exposing every imaginable body part to the golden rays. The background lilt hummed with the sounds of Italian, French, and Spanish.

The Biltmore is a small village dominated by a 315-foot tower that is a replica of Seville Cathedral's Giralda tower. There are multiple venues for dining, relaxing, and exercising, and the 19th Hole Golf Emporium serves delicious sandwiches for lunch. There we met a professor from the University of Miami and with him, as he said, "My wealthy, money-making friends, all originally from Lake Wobegon." He acclaimed the climate—sunny and warm in winter, and breezy and hot in the summer.

The Biltmore is only a short ten-minute ride to Miami's most famous landmark, Vizcaya. Here we found a Renaissance Italian villa with a striking formal garden. Vizcaya is in the midst of a mangrove swamp on the edge of Biscayne Bay. The stark contrast between the mangrove swamp and the orderly, planned villa and garden echoes the gulf between civilization and the state of nature.

Vizcaya was the dream child of James Deering (1859–1925), a wealthy industrialist from Chicago. His father, William, had founded the Deering Harvester Company, which in 1901 had nine thousand workers making binders, reapers, mowers, tractors, and corn harvesters. In 1906 Deering Harvester was merged by J. P. Morgan with the older and larger McCormick Company to form International Harvester Company. The Deering share of original issue was more than eight hundred million in today's dollars—the Deerings were suddenly very rich. James Deering as a young man had traveled extensively in Spain, France, Germany and Italy. He was now vice president of International Harvester. With his newfound wealth, he used antique firms in Florence, Italy, to assist him in procuring statues, tapestries, marble mantles, monumental garden fountains, and historic wrought-iron gates from Verona and Messina. These he stored in a warehouse in New York City. James at times visited his parents in Coconut Grove, Florida (south of Miami) then a small town of about ten thousand, and he had considered Egypt and the French Riviera in his search for the choice spot for a winter home. In contrast Biscayne Bay was a wild and savage place on the edge of the American frontier. James was an admirer of Ponce de Leon and the great Spanish and Portuguese explorers in general. He envisioned a mating of the Old World of Italy and Spain with the new American frontier in his villa and garden, which he called Vizcaya.

The villa was modeled on Villa Rezzonico at Bassano del Grappa in the Veneto countryside near Verona. Deering's Vizcaya had a square layout, an open central *cortile,* and twin turrets fronting the azure waters of Biscayne Bay. He designed each room to hold the many architectural masterpieces that were stored in New York City. Especially appealing is the second-floor breakfast room that overlooks the Italian garden through an open loggia. Here Deering and his friends were served royally from an adjacent kitchen. Today a glass roof has been placed over the central *cortile.* Its three arched windows look out on Biscayne Bay. In Deering's day soft and gentle breezes swept in from the bay, cooling the entire villa. He placed a stone island breakfront as a focal point from his eastern terrace, which faces the ocean. Here he docked his boats: his forty-foot-long cruiser built for speed, the *Psyche,* and his eighty-foot-long yacht, the *Nepanthe,* with comfortable living quarters for cruising and fishing on the Florida Keys.

The villa and garden at Vizcaya were envisioned as one, the perfection of Renaissance Italian style. Diego Suarez (1888–1974), the landscape architect for the garden, had studied landscape design in Florence at the Accademia di Belle Arti. He took James Deering to his favorite Italian garden, Villa Lante, near Viterbo, the sixteenth-century creation of landscape architect Giacomo Barozzi da Vignola. Suarez also took Deering to meet Lord Arthur Acton, who was restoring Villa Pietra on Via del Bologna in Florence. Suarez's design for Vizcaya includes elements of both Italian gardens. The one thousand or so workmen on site mined coral locally

The water staircase, Vizcaya, Miami, Florida

and created a hillside, called "the mound." The southern terrace of the villa looks over a fan-shaped garden toward the mound, which is topped with an Italian "casino" with sitting rooms and a fire place. The casino is a perfect garden room providing a vista of the garden. From it we enjoyed the water staircase, or runnel, that leads to a pool that then leads the eye through green parterres back to the terrace. This clever design provides the southern exposure of Vizcaya with a green and shaded focal point, away from the glare of Biscayne Bay. Like its Italian counterparts, the garden at Vizcaya is composed of stairways, balustrades, statues, paths, and green shrubs, with nary a flower in sight.

December in southern Florida is the dry season, a time when tropical flowers are blooming in a profusion of corals, pinks, oranges, and whites. We found this lush abundance at Fairchild Tropical Botanic Garden. Our tour guide, the senior horticulturist Mary Collins, knew the name of every exotic plant. The garden was named for Dr. David Fairchild (1869–1964). He had traveled the world in search of plants of potential use to the American people, finding mangos, alfalfa, soy beans, nectarines, and cherry trees. We smelled the sweet aromas from the leaves and flowers of vanilla, spice, and bay rum. Fairchild retired to Miami in 1935, and, along with Robert Montgomery (1872–1953), a banker, and William Lyman Phillips (1885–1966), a landscape architect, created Fairchild garden. The 83-acre garden consists of eight lakes, greenswards and more than 152 separate plots for similar botanical species. We especially enjoyed the rain forest with dense shade from trees and vines. Lavender, pink, and white orchids clung to tree trunks intermixed with staghorn ferns. The garden was filled with plants that attract butterflies, lizards, and hummingbirds. This was a day to enjoy nature, and not one to think about the troubles of the world. The Latin inscription from Horace's C.III.8.27–28 on the centerpiece of Vizcayas's chief façade comes to mind: "Dona praesentis cape laetus horae lingue serera" (Happily seize the gifts of the present hour; abandon grave things."

If you go:
Biltmore, Coral Gables, www.biltmorehotel.com (Tel. 305-445-8066)

Vizcaya Museum and Gardens, www.vizcayamuseum.org (Tel. 305-250-9133)

Fairchild Tropical Botanic Garden, www.fairchildgarden.org (Tel. 305-667-1651)

Paul Bennett, *The Garden Lover's Guide to the South*

Beyond Disney

A Taste of Florida's Orlando

DATE PALMS WAVED IN THE BREEZE OFF GRAND LAKES. Nearby, queen palms danced, luring me to join in their fun. Orlando is a great place to look for the charms of early 1900s Florida and to bask in the sun and tropical environment of our southernmost state.

When we arrived, an orange sun sank slowly into the black water swamps of Shingle Creek. This is Grande Lakes, Ritz Carlton, located on five hundred acres in the Florida wilderness. The lake that edges the Greg Norman golf course is alive with bass and tilapia. White ibis and blue heron gently stalk their prey, while the eyes of an alligator look mournfully aloof. The grounds are a showcase of palms, bamboo, and pink Brazilian silk trees. Butterflies and bees swarm the flowers of the purple passion vine. The multiple swimming pools are joined by a fast flowing "river" for floating through lush vegetation and under several waterfalls. The pungent scent of blooming ginger filled the air.

We journeyed to Orlando, not to be dazzled by Disney, but to explore the culture of those who wintered in Florida at the turn of the twentieth century. Our destinations were Winter Park, in order to see the Louis Comfort Tiffany (1848–1933) collection at the Morse Museum; Lake Wales, to see the Bok Tower Garden and "singing" carillon; and Jacksonville, to visit the Cummer Garden and Museum on the banks of the St. Johns River.

The Bok Tower Garden in Lake Wales is an easy forty-minute drive south of Orlando. Edward Bok (1863–1930), a publishing magnate and editor of *Ladies Home Journal,* came to central Florida in the early 1920s. He made his home on Mountain Lake near Iron Mountain, a 295-foot sand outcropping. Here he indulged his fantasy by building a 205-foot tower of pink and gray Georgia marble to house a carillon. Lighthouses, bell towers, and church steeples hold a fascination for me. I gazed down from the top of this 205-foot Gothic bell tower at a pastoral scene of citrus groves and a black-water lake protected by two white swans. Today the Bok Tower "prince" is Bill De Turk, the carillon keeper. Bill played a special concert for us and then let me play the bells, from the tinkling fifteen-pound high bell to the twenty-four-ton bass bell. The carillon was invented in Belgium in the 1500s as a means to alert villagers to the perils of fire, death, or an approaching army. Here it provides hourly musical interludes for those visiting the gardens. As we left the tower, I looked back to see light glinting from the polished brass door. Its surface was etched with the biblical story of creation.

The Bok Tower Garden on Lake Wales near Orlando, Florida

The Bok Tower Garden lives up to Edward Bok's life motto: "Make ye the world a bit better or more beautiful because you have lived in it." The garden was designed by the Olmsted firm of Boston, and it reflects the stewardship of William Lyman Phillips, who oversaw its development. Hurricane Charlie felled 79 of the biggest trees in 2004. Today the garden chief, Nick Baker, tends a magnificent garden of camellias and azaleas that bloom in January and February. Nick was particularly proud of the enormous pink Amazonia water lilies whose circles grace the black waters of the lake below the carillon.

We meandered down the hillside for a tour of Pinewood, a formal garden and house set in the midst of the 250-acre Bok estate. The Arts and Crafts house was the home of steel magnate Charles Austin Buck (1867–1945). The garden is strongly Italianate with crossing axis of clipped and domed citrus trees. The house is filled with decorative tiles. The back terrace looks onto a walled garden with a moon-gate as a central focal point. The Pinewood house and garden are decorated each year for Christmas.

Winter Park, the home of the Morse Museum, is another place to find the Florida culture of the early 1900s. The Morse Museum houses a treasure trove of sparkling glass lamps, vases, windows, and doors, all created in the Louis Comfort Tiffany Glassworks. In addition there are splendid paintings by Tiffany himself. Tiffany (1848–1933) pioneered art glass, including glass tiles, molded glass, and leaded-glass windows. His goal was to create a total interior design effect. The Morse collection has an iridescent impact, like walking through a kaleidoscope. The centerpiece of the collection is the chapel, which Tiffany created for the world's Columbian Exposition held in Chicago in 1893. The biblical panels are lustrous. The entire collection is extensive and was assembled from the remains of Tiffany's summer home Laurelton, at Oyster Bay on Long Island. Tiffany's inspiration was the natural world. We made a seamless transition from the brilliance of Tiffany's creations to the Harry P. Leu Garden, also in Winter Park. There we found a tropical abundance of yellow hibiscus, pink princess flower, purple beautyberry, and coral bougainvillea.

Charleston to Orlando is a seven-hour drive. We broke the drive home to enjoy Amelia Island and Jacksonville. The Ritz on Amelia Island overlooks the ocean and features the Spice Band every Saturday night for those who love to waltz and shag.

The Cummer Museum and Garden, on the banks of the St. Johns River, Jacksonville, Florida

The Cummer Garden and Museum on the St. Johns River in Jacksonville is a nearby destination for discovering Florida culture from another era. The Cummer brothers were timber barons from Michigan who settled on the St. Johns long before an interstate rumbled through their secluded neighborhood. The museum has an extensive collection of Meissen plates, bowls, and figurines. It also houses a fine collection of nineteenth-century American paintings by George Inness, Benjamin West, Thomas Sully, Herman Herzog, Edmund Darch Lewis, and Winslow Homer. The formal gardens extend along the river frontage and include an Italianate garden after that of Villa Gamberaia in Fiesole and an English garden of roses and perennial borders.

Finding the culture of early 1900s Florida requires a focus that allows one to see quality without over exposure to "sideshows." The Flagler railroad brought the rich and famous of an earlier generation to Florida, and their handiwork is still there to enjoy along with the sun and the luxurious semitropical environment of the new Florida.

If you go:
www.boktowergardens.org; www.grandelakes.com; www.cummer.org; www.morsemuseum.org; www.ritzcarlton.com/en/Properties/Ameliaisland

Steven Brooke, *The Gardens of Florida*

An Adventure in Art

Cà d'Zan, the Ringling Estate in Sarasota, Florida

THE GULFSIDE ESTATE OF JOHN (1866–1936) and Mable (1875–1929) Ringling (married in 1905) is a multilayered experience in art. Exploring each of these vibrant facets provides a fun-filled adventure. On a blustery, sunny day, we entered the Gothic portal. The entrance pavilion was alive with visitors from all over the world. Florida "in season" is truly an international venue. We exchanged salutations with two couples from Munich. We sat in the sun with a blond-haired, blue-eyed family from the Netherlands. With sixty-six acres, the Ringling Estate absorbs a crowd easily. The estate is meticulously maintained and shows the skillful management of Florida State University.

Our first destination was the circular wagon-wheel rose garden that had been the pride of Mable Ringling. There we met Kevin Greene, the landscape superintendent, and his assistant Loretta. Roses in every shade of pink, vermillion, red, and yellow danced in the strong breeze. Pigmy palms accent the corners of the wheel design, while deep-green banyan trees provide a screen from the Sarasota Bay. On the day of our visit, gulls and pelicans soared overhead, enlivening the garden with their mews and cries. Kevin told us that gardening in the Florida climate was a daunting challenge.

Most think of Florida as a tropical oasis. Yet a climate that runs the gamut from a summer high of 110 degrees to a winter low of 28 degrees has a full array of pests and fungi. The rose bushes were deep green and sturdy, showing no sign of the lurking plague of mildew, black spot, and Chilean Tripe. Kevin noted that a county commissioner's edict (to prevent red tide in the bay) mandated no phosphorus or nitrogen fertilizers from June 1st through October. Loretta laughed that come 11:59 on May 31st a crowd of volunteers assisted her in applying Florican, a six-month fertilizer. The results of quality gardening were stunning, with an exotic array of velvety, luscious blooms. The "rose of the day" was "Stainless Steel," gray-colored with a lavender tint and a lemony perfume.

We left the roses for a tour of Cà d'Zan, the Gothic mansion that sits on the edge of the Bay and that was designed to look like a Venetian palazzo. Our tour guide, Phyllis, told us that the mansion had cost $1.5 million when built in 1924, and that the renovation (1995–2001) had amounted to an additional $15 million. The pristine quality of each splendid room showed that money makes a difference. I could imagine dancing in the ballroom, whose ceiling was painted with the *Dancers of the Nations* by Willy Pogany, a Hollywood set designer. I sensed the delight of a

The John and Mable Ringling Museum on the gulf at Sarasota, Florida

Ringling cocktail party in the central court with its marble floors and onyx columns. The greatest thrill was Ringling's palatial bedroom, with his well-stocked closet of pointed leather shoes, white suits, and brimmed hats. Fred was more tempted by the life-sized seminude painting of Pauline Bonaparte Borghese. Each room shines with Delft porcelains, gold-encased clocks, sparkling chandeliers, and period furniture acquired by Ringling at New York City auctions and through purchases in Venice and Florence. The hand-blown window panes of lavender, pink, and blue create a warm glow throughout the interior of the house, and the twelve thousand-foot marble terrace by the gulf gives access to a tile-covered pier, the docking place for Ringling's 125-foot luxury yacht, the *Zalophus*. The sun was intense, the sky blue, and the terrace provided the perfect place for enjoying the ambience of a mid-winter Florida view of the gulf. Some great houses leave me feeling poignant among the memories of the lives of another era. Cà d'Zan with its exuberance and inviting hospitality made me feel as though I were an invited guest for a weekend of frivolity, pleasure, and passion.

Sarasota is such a beautiful and luxurious cultural destination. The Ringling Estate has a superb art museum and two theaters for musical and dramatic performances. One could spend a day or a week being entertained by the cultural events. The museum opened in 1930 and is just the right size for a stroll of several hours. Its two wings encompass a fountain and statue-filled courtyard. Ringling was an avid collector. In 1926 Ringling purchased three rooms of paintings, furniture, and architectural furnishings from the Astor Mansion on 65th St. and Fifth Avenue in New York City. In 1928 he purchased more than twenty-eight hundred Greek, Roman, and Egyptian antiquities from the Metropolitan Museum of Art in New York. The museum houses an enormous collection of religious art, with the especially fine *The Triumph of the Eucharist* by Peter Paul Rubens.

Sarasota is a great February retreat from most U.S. climes. We stayed on the gulf at the Sarasota Ritz, which has extensive sea vistas, along with the amenities of a heated pool and great workout facilities. The fun of the Ringling Estate is that in one lovely location one can enjoy a fantastic house museum, a quality rose garden, a delicious meal at the Verona Restaurant, attend a play at the Asolo Theater, and a stroll through a quality museum.

If you go: www.ritz-carlton.com; 1111 Ritz-Carlton Drive, Sarasota, Fla. 34236 (Tel. 942-309-2000); www.ringling.org

Touring the Hudson
River Valley in Fall

WHAT BETTER WAY TO SEE the famed Hudson River Valley than with the Historic Charleston Foundation? Friday dawned brilliant, and on arrival at Newark we set out for Mohonk Resort, the remains of the ten-thousand-acre Quaker Preserve in the Shawangunk Mountains. The six-hundred-room Victorian castle sits atop a mountain ledge. We settled into a comfortable lounge where tea and cookies were being served, and there was a huge roaring fire. Carriage paths surrounded the lake, which had ruffled white caps from the strong northwest wind.

The next morning arrived cold, wet, and windy, as we visited the William Frederick Vanderbilt Mansion on a bluff on the Hudson River in Duchess County. With raincoats and umbrellas we were the lone guests in the Italian garden with its roses and begonias dripping water and its fountains and marble statues stark against the gray sky. Inside was warm, splendid, and unexpectedly inviting. Lit by old gas lamps and chandeliers, the place is comfortable with rose and blue oriental rugs, matching velvet chairs and sofas, and unique marbles and bronzes. Frederick William Vanderbilt (1856–1938) was a grandson of the famous commodore who made his fortune from steamboats and railroads. Frederick and his beautiful wife, Louise Anthony, used the Hudson Valley home in Hyde Park as a fall and spring retreat from the social life of New York City and Newport.

We left the Vanderbilt Mansion for Rhinebeck, a small Victorian village where we stayed in the charming Delamater Inn. Olana, our first destination, has a breathtaking 180-degree view of the Hudson River Valley. Clouds and sun mixed a palette of green, blue, and yellow so familiar in the paintings of Frederick Edwin Church (1826–1900), whose Olana is a house with an amalgamation of Middle Eastern ceramics, braziers, minarets, arches, and views of the countryside. Church was the sole student of Thomas Cole (1801–1848), whose house is across the river in the Catskills. Two of Cole's allegorical paintings adorn the house, including one with a moonrise over the Anglican graveyard in Rome. There are splendid Church paintings there: Mount Ida with its mauve tinted sky above black mountains; the gold fishbowl painted for his children; the two memorial paintings of the rising sun and rising moon to commemorate the death of his two oldest children of diphtheria; exquisite landscapes with setting suns; and a chromolithograph of an iceberg, used to authenticate his enormous iceberg painting. The setting is rich with tapestries and old oriental rugs. Outside in the sunny walled garden, the squeaks of chipmunks and the chirp of dying crickets combine with the pipe of wrens in a garden palette of blues (delphiniums), yellow and oranges (zinnias, gaillardias), pinks (hollyhocks), and the lingering sweet perfume of honeysuckle. We departed Olana for Montgomery Place. The driveway to the federal-style mansion is through an avenue of black locust trees. From the front porch we looked across meadows to the Hudson River. There are more than eight "designed vistas," creating a spectacle of river, sky, and land. The house takes full advantage of its setting.

The house has been owned since 1988 by the New-York Historical Society. Edgewater, our next destination, is one of the homes of Richard Jenrette, the New York stockbroker and collector of grand Belle Epoque city homes and plantations. It was built about 1804. There are pristine views from every window, and a front portico with Doric columns. Jenrette has recovered the original Duncan Phyfe furniture, and today it is restored with green and aqua silks that pick up the colors of the exterior lawns. Each room has mirrors, portraits, clocks, and silver of the early nineteenth century. A portrait of George Washington is over the mantel while a French George Washington gilt clock chimes the hours. All the walls are faux white marble and look like quarried marble. There is a small classical temple on the edge of the property that is gleaming white and adorned with a full set of the twenty lithographs of Henry Megarey from 1820 that show the Hudson River in all its pristine glory.

The morning dawned brilliant with frost on the grass. Our destination was Cold Spring, whose evocative name comes from the fact that George Washington drank water from a wonderful cold spring in the region. Our first stop was Boscobel, the 1804 home of States Dyckman (1755–1806). The delicate Duncan Phyfe furniture dates from 1790 and was made in England. Each room is set as it would have been in Dyckman's time. The sitting room is ready for music with a harpsichord and flute. The dining room has two Duncan Phyfe sideboards, one whose knives are contained in a Roman sarcophagus-styled box. The candelabra, for which Dykeman paid five thousand dollars, reflects light from the girandole mirrors.

The inspiration for the home, furnishing, and art objects was the 1740s rediscovery of Pompeii and Herculaneum. There is an atrium-designed entry hall with classical prints of Roman ruins and of Mercury and Venus. The house re-creates the ways of living prevalent in the early nineteenth century. There are grand lamps of exquisite silver that are cleaned daily to prevent smoke. In the kitchen there are spits for cooking over an open fire, a bread oven, and a Wellington stove that cooks by reflected heat from the fire. One truly felt as one would have with the Dyckmans in this elegant but livable home. The exterior has a belvedere from which the whole panorama of the Hudson escarpments and West Point are visible.

October 7 dawned a cold 34 degrees, and fog blanketed the fields. We drove just out of Rhinebeck along the bronze-tinted road to Wildstein, the home of the Buckley family from 1852 to 1983, with substantial enlargements being made to the structure in 1888. Open only on Thursday to Sunday, noon to 4 P.M., its five-story tower and Victorian filigree millwork evoke the Victorian homes of Flat Rock, North Carolina. The wicker furniture on the porch rocks with memories of bygone days. Sitting high on a hill above the Hudson, the vistas were eerie with fog and mist rising from the river.

At each of these historic mansions a central theme is the intermingling of landscape and home. Wonderful vistas are brought into the home by various design strategies. Homes and mansions are positioned to capture sunlight and moonlight, with windows carefully placed to bring in views of meadows, river, Catskill Mountains, clouds, sunrise, and sunset. Gardens have been created and designed to produce cut flowers for the table and for afternoon strolls.

A final extravaganza was a four-course dinner at the Escoffier at the CIA, or Culinary Institute of America. Once a Jesuit monastery, the splendid setting over the Hudson amplifies the importance of the place in the culinary world. The four-course dinner is a taster's dream, served perfectly by legions of young, attentive students. Round tables for six are set with spotless linen, crystal, and silverware. We began with two lobster claws on a lovely round of avocado topped with cream lobster sauce, and the accompanying white wine was delicate and smooth. That was followed by salmon en croûte. Then, with a sound of trumpets, six waiters appeared behind our chairs with silver serving covers and in unison removed and placed before us three savory, rare loin lamb chops. They had been smeared in mustard, then dipped in seasoned bread crumbs and grilled. The magnificent morel sauce was a perfect accompaniment, and the red merlot had a hint of raspberry. The final treat was an apple tart. Satiated, we waddled away from the feast.

Our last destination was a visit to Kykuit, the Rockefeller estate in Tarrytown. The estate is dramatic, sitting on a hilltop with a distant view of the Hudson River. Built by John D. Rockefeller in 1909, it was modified by John D. Rockefeller, Jr., in 1913, and lived in eventually by Governor Nelson Rockefeller and his wife, Happy. The Italian garden and the rose garden were beautifully designed, full of marble focal points and well-clipped box.

The estate is entered through two magnificent forty-foot gates topped with pineapples. One end is anchored by the house, the other by a gigantic fountain ensemble representing Oceanus and the Three Rivers. Lovely, matching water parterres gurgle on either side of the entry path.

If you go:
Boscobel, Cold Spring (Tel. 845-265-3638) or www.boscobel.org

Brandow's, Hudson, N.Y. (Tel. 518-822-8938) or
www.brandowsandcompany.com

The Culinary Institute of America, Hyde Park (Tel. 845-471-6608) or www.ciachef.edu

Cripple Creek, Rhinebeck, N.Y. (Tel. 845-876-4355) or www.cripplecreekrestaurant.com

Dupuy Canal House, High Falls, N.Y. (Tel. 845-687-7700)

Montgomery Place, Annandale-on-Hudson, N.Y. (Tel. 845-758-5461) or www.hudsonvalley.org

Marist College, Poughkeepsie (Tel. 914-575-3000) or www.marist.edu

Manitoga, Garrison, N.Y. (Tel. 914-424-3812) or manitoga@highlands.com

Mohonk Resort, New Paltz, N.Y. (Tel. 845-255-1000 or 800-678-8946)

Vanderbilt Mansion, Hyde Park, N.Y. (Tel. 845-229-9115) or www.nps.gov/vama

Elisabeth Donaghy Garrett, *At Home: The American Family, 1750–1870*

Visiting Philadelphia

TWO OF MY BOOKS, *An Antebellum Plantation Household* and *Between North and South,* are as much about Philadelphia as Charleston and the South Carolina lowcountry. Philadelphia of the late nineteenth and early twentieth centuries was a place of culture, distinction, and money. Today that Philadelphia aristocracy of Biddles, Cadwaladers, Peppers, Roosevelts, Coxes, Sinklers, and Whartons has retreated into the wealthy suburbs of a once-proud city. While we do not often take a group tour, there are benefits of access to private homes. Our visit to Philadelphia was with the Historic Charleston Foundation.

The Philadelphia of today is a city of 1.5 million. Germantown was once a delightful summer suburb. Cliveden House, a National Historic Landmark, sits on two green acres. A tour of the house that had been inhabited by seven generations of the same family gave me a feeling of nostalgia. This is a house that time and family have left behind. The scene of the Revolutionary War battle of Germantown, it is today but a memory of the past. The elegant houses of Fairmont Park, Mt. Pleasant, Lemon Hill, and Cedar Hill all sit on the hill above the Schuylkill River. Mt. Pleasant is the most impressive. Because of renovations and the need for a new roof, the house sits much like Drayton Hall, to which it has been compared, unfurnished. Built in 1762 by a Scottish sea captain and American patriot, the elegant house in Georgian style features some of the finest surviving examples of Philadelphia architectural carving of its time. Today there are plans to revive the once-proud gardens and give the house a view of the river and city.

The wealth, culture, and pre-eminence of Philadelphia are solidly ensconced in the Philadelphia Museum of Art. The museum houses a fine collection of American nineteenth-century art. Our tour paid special attention to elegant period rooms from the nineteenth century that showcase Philadelphia furniture, fine arts, and portraiture. Thomas Sully (1783–1872) painted the images of the wealthy merchants and gentlemen whose houses in Society Hill were the center of Philadelphia wealth and power. Exquisite silver, casement clocks, and period furniture are a reminder that the most expert of American craftsmen worked in Philadelphia.

That afternoon we sallied forth for an afternoon of exploring the Philadelphia countryside. We drove through the darkening country and pulled through tight gates into Androssan, an estate reminiscent of Philadelphia's baronial aristocracy. We were met by Robert Montgomery Scott, the fourth in line to inherit his family's estate. The mahogany-paneled living room contains the vestiges of bygone days, with portraits of faces from the past, and the exquisitely crewel-worked sofas and chairs have the handprint of earlier elegance. In the music room, where our host told us tales from his past, an open bar and specialty wines and cheeses added to the ambience. An air of anticipation was rewarded when the dinner bell sounded. We were taken into another mahogany-paneled room with a table set for twenty-five, with old silver, china, and crystal. The dinner began with cold salmon and white wine, which was followed by chicken cordon bleu and topped off with cherry pie and ice cream. Our toasts to our host echoed through this enormous Georgian brick manor house.

The next morning we set forth to the banks of the Delaware River and the famous James Biddle (1783–1848) estate of Andalusia. The Biddles still live in this lovely green enclave. Here we could see that fall was touching the Pennsylvania countryside with its orange, red, and yellow hues. We were treated to a private tour of the interior where marble busts of Aphrodite mingle with Wedgwood porcelain and period furniture. We dined in a small garden al fresco with delicious sandwiches provided by a local gourmet shop.

Despite their elegance and charm, both Andalusia and Ardrossan seem remote vestiges of a world that is gone. Is it possible to live in the museums of the past? As we look around the lowcountry of South Carolina, we do have examples of old estates that remain vital: Mulberry, Medway, and Halidon Hill are a few of our country estates that continue to carry on the traditions of our own South Carolina lowcountry. Within our own center city, there is a vibrancy and polish that rings with today's lifestyle.

If you go:
The best place to stay in Philadelphia to enjoy the entire city center experience is the Rittenhouse Hotel; www.rittenhousehotel.com, 210 West Rittenhouse Square.

The Highlands, a forty-four-acre historic site at Fort Washington, Pennsylvania, with its late eighteenth-century Georgian mansion and two-acre formal garden, descended from Carolina Sinkler to Nicholas and Emily Roosevelt and is now administered as a charitable trust open to the public; www.highlandshistorical.org.

Robert F. Looney, *Old Philadelphia in Early Photographs 1839–1914*

Finding an Angel in New Orleans, and Diversions along the Way

"YOU GOT TO KNOW WHEN TO HOLD 'EM; know when to fold 'em. Know when to walk away; know when to run."

Yes, Johnny Cash, an auction in New Orleans is a good crap shoot, a fine gamble, and exciting, especially when you can "just walk away" from Neal's Gallery with a "Guardian Angel." Neal's guardian angel fit well into the iconography of good angels, not the fallen or Lucifer type. Its spreading wings offer protection to a vulnerable mortal. Almost five feet tall and created in a foundry in Italy, this angel exemplifies the fine range of bronzes, marbles, paintings, and ceramics that one can find at the auctions in the major New Orleans galleries: New Orleans, Neal and St. Charles. These auction houses enjoy a fine reputation for their extensive and lovely collections of antiques and fine arts.

Bidding at auctions today is relatively easy. Telephone and internet bids work well as do "left" bids. Shipping can be easily arranged with FedEx or UPS. However, when you have purchased a 128-pound angel, the challenge of retrieval is somewhat greater. What better reason for a journey to New Orleans than to pick it up?

A drive to New Orleans from Charleston, all eleven hours of it, can become like an afternoon ride in the country. It is simply a matter of attitude and a question of appropriate diversions and destinations along the way. Crossing the Edisto, the Cumbahee, and the Ashepoo along Highway 17 reminded me that the South Carolina coast has water fingers that meander through exquisite marshland alive with gulls, pelicans, and kingfishers.

How best to while away the hours on such a long drive? Each landmark on I-10 brought a song to mind. As we crossed the rolling hills of the Florida panhandle, the roiling Suwannee River (flowing southerly from the Okeefenokee Swamp slicing the panhandle) evoked Stephen Foster's 1851 "Old Folks at Home": "Way down upon de Swanee ribber, Far, far away, Dere's wha my heart is turning ebber, Dere's wha de old folks stay."

Entry into Alabama stirred memories of Mitchell Parish's 1934 "Stars Fell on Alabama," which evokes the Leonid meteor shower of 1833:

> We lived our little drama,
> we kissed in a field of white,
> and stars fell on Alabama last night.

. . . .

My heart beat like a hammer,
my arms wound around you tight,
and stars fell on Alabama last night."

Before we knew it, we had arrived at our destination, Fairhope, Alabama, and the Grand Hotel. The Grand Hotel sits on a point looking south into Mobile Bay. The water-lapped location and manicured grounds are welcoming after a long drive. We watched the sun set into the bay against a lavender and purple sky, and then we settled into one of the many swings to watch the stars. The stars seemed to hang on sticks. The cool night air soon drew us to one of the blazing fire pits that dot the grounds of the Grand Hotel. Other friendly souls were there enjoying evening cocktails. Early the next morning I toured the grounds with Niall Frazier, the chief gardener. He told me how the oaks had been pruned and fertilized after Katrina. One especially towering oak grows around and through a huge camellia. With more than eighty weddings a year at three different outdoor "chapels," the grounds are always brightly planted with annuals, roses, and perennials.

New Orleans is an easy two-hour ride from Fairhope. We stopped along the way at Bellingrath Garden, ten miles south of Mobile, and listened to the splashing sounds of water rills and cascades in the memorable formal water gardens found riverside. Situated on the Fowl River, Bellingrath was originally a fishing camp, but it was transformed in the 1930s into a camellia haven.

A highlight of any trip to New Orleans is a walk around beautiful Audubon Park. The park is a watery oasis for wood ducks, and their eerie cry fills the evening air. The glistening backs of turtles shine on fallen limbs. White egrets balance beautifully among the American cypress trees. Over it all towers the cathedral on the Tulane campus.

LongVue is another New Orleans house and garden that is always worth a visit. The water gardens were created by the owner Edith Stern (1895–1980) after a visit to the Generalife garden at the Alhambra in Granada. There are rills, jets, canals, and small water focal points framed by a green avenue of grass. The Spanish court that she created has twelve side fountains, including a classical dolphin fountain that she purchased from Seville. The walks are paved with French tiles and are accented by polished Mexican pebbles embedded on edge in patterns taken from walks in Barcelona. This garden is full of camellias in February and is lush with old oak trees with gray moss.

Our destination on the trip back to Charleston was the Ritz Carlton on Amelia Island. As we pulled into the hotel driveway, the melodies of the Island Spice Band made us realize that the dancing and drinking hour had arrived. We quickly donned appropriate attire and were soon shagging. Dinner that evening at Salt, the premier restaurant, was memorable for the tempting orange sauce prepared to adorn rack of lamb. We went to sleep lulled by the dim roar of crashing waves and in the sure knowledge that Charleston was but a mere three-hour drive home the next day.

If you go:
The Grand Hotel. Point Clear, Alabama (Tel. 251-928-9201). The Grand has three golf courses as well as indoor and outdoor swimming pools.

The Ritz Carlton, 4750 Amelia Island Parkway, Amelia Island, Florida (Tel. 904-277-1100). www.bellingrathgarden.com

Epilogue

Stories and Memories

MY MOTHER, EMILY WHALEY (1911–1998), liked to say that we have a gardening gene in our family. My spin on our gardening proclivity is that, from generation to generation, the women in our family have loved the land and sought beauty and inspiration by designing and cultivating gardens. Our men tilled the land; we turned the land into gardens.

Our families' earliest remembered gardening tradition started six generations ago. On the banks of the Delaware River, around 1800, Mary Core Griffith created a garden that was pungent with the sweet aroma and perfume of hundreds of old-fashioned roses. On a warm spring day the glorious huge fruitlike blooms fashioned a rainbow of pinks, mauves, crimsons, blood red, velvety rose, tangerine, and yellow. The garden was alive with the song of birds—wrens, thrushes, red birds, and mocking birds. All around were the humming and buzzing of bees. Mary Core Griffith named her plantation Charlie's Hope, and all her money was spent on this place, where she planted acres of roses in rows, like corn, for her bees. It is said she spent twenty-five thousand dollars on her apiary alone.

Mary Core Griffith's garden was the summer playground of her Philadelphia-bred granddaughter, Emily Wharton (1823–1875), my great-great grandmother. In this idyllic landscape, free from the city cares of Philadelphia in the 1830s, Emily learned to love the carefully crafted spaces of her grandmother's garden. Her love and knowledge of roses grew with each year. Indeed, when she married Charles Sinkler (1818–1894) of South Carolina in September of 1842, legend has it that Emily wore a wreath of her favorite roses, Souvenir de Malmaison, twined through her thick curly dark hair.

Emily and Charles moved into the Sinkler family's ancestral home, Belvidere, in 1848; it was located on the banks of the Santee River in lower South Carolina. Charles gave Emily a gardener and a carpenter, and she set about restoring a garden that still had its shape, or footprint, but had not been planted for almost four decades. Emily wrote home, "It is now nearly 40 years since it was tended but it contains many shrubs yet. I have arranged a small garden on each side of the front steps which is enclosed with an iron fence and is to contain the choicest specimens." Emily tells of "foraging all through the country for roots and cuttings." And she talks of her roses: "The Glory of France, Harrisonian de Brunnius, Cloth of Gold, and Souvenir de Malmaison. This last is the most splendid rose you ever saw, as large as a coffee cup and so firm and rich."

Belvidere Plantation House, the home of the Charles Sinkler family, near Eutawville, South Carolina

Emily's beautiful iris walk with its rose hedges was truly glorious in the spring. Her annual beds of mignonette and heart's ease were bright with the colors of blue and pink, while the aroma of sweet tea olive suffused the air. The Belvidere garden was designed with a long central avenue. The avenue was covered by an arbor of Lady Bankshire and Cherokee roses, intertwined with panicles of wisteria. On one side were flower beds and paths lined with lilacs and crab apple trees. On the other side was a rich kitchen garden full of asparagus, spring peas, mushrooms, and spinach.

The Belvidere garden was inherited by Emily's daughter-in-law, Anne Wickham Porcher (1860–1919), who married my great-grandfather Charles St. George Sinkler (1853–1934). Anne's gift to the Belvidere garden was the wonderful rose and wisteria-covered arbors, the secret nooks, and secluded hideaways. Anne's partner in gardening was Daddy Lewis. When Anne died at the young age of fifty-four, Daddy Lewis grieved terribly, until one afternoon she appeared to him in a vision, saying, "Daddy Lewis, while you grieve so, my soul can find no rest. You must cease." And Daddy Lewis did.

Caroline "Carrie" Sydney Sinkler (1860–1949) went north after the Civil War to live at her place, the Highlands, in Ambler, Pennsylvania, outside of Philadelphia. There Carrie created a garden with broad lawns, sweeping vistas, wonderful arbors, and carefully designed beds of peonies, perennial phlox, and roses. Her

The author on the remains of the front steps of Belvidere House

garden was in many ways an echo of her mother Emily's Belvidere garden. The Highlands is in a historic trust today and is open to the public.

The Belvidere garden with its wonderful hideaways, surprising cul-de-sacs and perches for watching foxes, birds, and rabbits, became the playground of Anne Porcher Sinkler's daughters, Anne Sinkler Fishburne (Nan; 1886–1983) and her sisters Emily Sinkler Roosevelt (Em; 1884–1970) and Caroline Sinkler Lockwood (Cad). My grandmother Nan cared for the Belvidere garden until it was inundated in 1942 by the Santee Cooper impoundment that created Lake Marion. Nan and Em moved from Belvidere, but the memories of the garden of their youth went with them. Soon there were wonderful echoes of Belvidere at Em's Gippy Plantation garden outside of Moncks Corner, South Carolina, and Nan's thirteen-acre farm in Pinopolis, South Carolina.

My great-aunt Caroline Sidney Sinkler Lockwood (Cad; 1894–1993) settled with her husband, Dunbar Lockwood (1894–1967), on a Topsfield, Massachusetts, farm with an ancient house and a lovely garden. Adjacent to the garden were several large greenhouses for Dunbar's superb orchid collection, where he bred new and improved strains of showy orchids for his own pleasure and commercially. I remember so vividly and with such pleasure a visit with Aunt Cad and Uncle Dunny shortly after Fred and I were married. On a warm, bluebird day in July, we walked the extended paths through the forest and pastures of the farm. Then we were taken to the nearby shore for a bracing swim in the frigid waters of the North Atlantic Ocean. We came back and joined Uncle Dunny to pick Silver Queen corn and other vegetables for lunch from his garden. We helped drop the corn and string beans, picked just fifteen minutes before, into the pots next to the pot of boiling water into which Uncle Dunny released six or eight wiggling, freshly caught lobsters we had brought back with us from the shore. Following a delightful nap and rest period after lunch, we walked up over the hill for an exhilarating swim in the "skinny-dipping" lake in the late afternoon before returning to the house and garden for the cocktail hour. Although Aunt Cad and Uncle Dunny lived in the North, we saw them and various members of their family on their regular visits to South Carolina at Nan's farm and Aunt Em's Gippy Plantation.

We have had the satisfaction of getting to know, love, and break bread with many of our Lockwood kin: Dunbar Lockwood, Jr. (1927–2005), Grace Stackpole Lockwood (1923–1990), and Caroline Sidney Lockwood Tynan (Sidney; 1921–). We have enjoyed delightful visits with Sidney at her country place in Little Compton, Rhode Island, where she, true to Sinkler tradition, has a fine garden with lovely vistas and walks and where she up until a year or two ago was still riding her horses through the countryside.

Nan was a soil person. Gradually she filled her farm with a camellia garden, a rose garden, and a wild swamp garden full of azaleas, bay trees, and bamboo. Nan believed that gardens were an extension of the home, rooms to be enjoyed and sat in. She created places for sitting, reading, and listening to her harpies, the wind singing in her pine trees. There Nan and my mother, Emily Whaley, would sit together reading aloud or playing bridge. Both Mother's wedding reception and mine were held at Nan's farm, with guests spilling into the gardens and onto the broad lawns.

My aunt Anne Sinkler Fishburne (Peach; 1913–1983) and her husband, William Moultrie Ball (Moultrie; 1910–1997) lived across the main village road in Pinopolis, South Carolina, from Nan and Doc's farm. Peach and Moultrie's house has a lovely vista across Lake Moultrie and a garden filled with camellias and azaleas. Throughout her life, Peach assumed the responsibility of cutting the beautiful blooming flowers from Nan's different gardens and arranging them attractively as focal points in the sitting rooms and bedrooms of Nan's house. Peach joined Nan in their never-ending garden club projects to beautify the roadsides of the village of Pinopolis with various indigenous plants—such as dogwood, camellias, and azaleas—to enhance the quality of life in the community.

Peach's daughter Anne Moultrie Helms (Moonie) and her husband, William Collier Helms (Billy), are close family and friends. We spent most of our summers together at High Hills, the home built in Flat Rock, North Carolina, by my great-grandparents Charles St. George Sinkler and his wife, Anne Porcher Sinkler, in 1917. We used to sit on the porch of the Flat Rock house so many summer afternoons, talking as the curtain of darkness descended on the subtle, enchanted changes of color in the tree-framed vista to the Blue Ridge Mountains. We would watch for the chipmunks to make their crossings under the enormous granite slab which sat at the top of the stone stair to the terrace below the driveway into the tangles of ivy on either side of the stair. We would listen for the melodic eventide songs of the wrens in the lovely hillside garden, a greensward edged by large, old, carefully clipped English boxwoods. During my grandmother Nan's tenure, there were always dahlias for picking in the terraced garden.

As we all know, the lowcountry rain, sun, and a long growing season soon produce a jungle. Nan had no heart for pruning so she called on Mother for the annual clipping. Nan would have every blade on the place sharpened to a fine edge. Frank Williams, Nan's gardener, who loved to prune, would stand ready. Mother and Frank gleefully and judiciously pruned all day. Nan, who hated to cut anything, would soon retreat to the inside. At the end of the day, the jungle would be pushed back, once again showing the footprint of the garden plan.

Nan was a frugal person, reaping the rewards of her summer vegetable garden and brewing her own blackberry and scuppernong wine. Her blackberry wine was among the best in the lowcountry, and anyone who came to Nan's house was offered a taste of this elixir in one of her beautiful green Venetian glasses. Each spring Nan would send word through her cook, Catherine (Cat) Beatty, that she would buy all the plump, ripe blackberries anyone would bring her. Nan inherited her blackberry wine recipe from Grandmother Emily, and it is printed in *An Antebellum Plantation Household.*

Like many gardeners Nan was more than willing to share with anyone her love of creating with sun, earth, and water. Her sister Em's garden at Gippy was in Nan's care six months of the year while Em was at the Highlands in Philadelphia. Em's garden was another lovely echo of Grandmother Emily's garden at Belvidere. But Em had seen the fabled gardens of Florence and Rome. Her vistas were closely framed to focus on beautiful statues of Diana, Aphrodite, or Mercury. She too had her kitchen garden full of mushrooms and spinach. Her first words of greeting to her sister Nan on descent from the train were "Miss Anne, have you got my stand of spinach up yet?"

Em provided her garden with a solid brick wall edged on top with the prickly pear thorn tree. She believed that the garden wall not only gave privacy but kept the "haints" at bay. I remember as a girl of fourteen, perched out of sight, in a tree in Em's garden and watching as a beautiful white-tailed buck easily jumped the wall to enjoy the abundance of her kitchen garden. Em's large front lawn became the centerpiece of another of Nan's passions, an annual Berkeley County lancing tournament. For Nan the pageantry recalled the glory of Sir Walter Scott and similar lancing tournaments held at Pineville, South Carolina.

My mother, Emily Whaley, liked to say that any good garden must begin with a plan. Her own garden plan at 58 Church Street was the result of my birth. She had been put in bed flat on her back when she was five months pregnant. My father,

Ben Scot Whaley (1909–1987), seeing her discomfort, asked what he could do to make her happy. Her instant answer was a Loutrel Briggs (1893–1977) design for her garden.

Emily Whaley often said that, when she was in her garden, she never felt alone. She was at one with her soul in her garden with its constantly changing patterns of light and shade, the visible growth of plants and flowers, the sounds of bees, and her flock of doves. It was here that she escaped what she considered to be an over-scheduled world. It was here that she caught up with her soul. She loved to tell the story of a group of well-to-do American men on safari in Africa. Once there they set off in a cloud of dust, with a fury for the hunting grounds, their porters following on foot. The third day of the trek there was a resounding stillness behind them. When inquiring why, the lead porter was told that the men had to sit and wait a while for their souls to catch up with them. For Mother this was a parody on today's overpaced, overscheduled state. For her the garden was the perfect antidote.

Emily Whaley believed that the "bones of a garden" are critical. She spent a lifetime with the garden design at 58 Church Street of Loutrel Briggs. But she was not just a successful gardener. She became an accomplished vernacular garden designer and was always willing to offer counsel on garden design when asked by her friends in Charleston. She, Sally (Mrs. Creighton Frampton; ?–1964), and Sarah Lee (Mrs. Frederick Richards) oversaw the maintenance and planting of the garden at the Historic Charleston Foundation's Russell House for much of their lives.

When Major General John Grinalds was president of the Citadel, his wife, Norwood, became very concerned by construction of buildings that compromised the vista over the Ashley River marsh from the president's quarters and garden on the Citadel campus. She talked with Emily Whaley about the problem, and Emily came up immediately with a remedy: "Buy the three biggest magnolias you can find with root-balls so large they can be moved and planted only by the large mechanized plant-mover trucks." Today the tranquility of the vista is no longer disturbed by unsightly buildings but is anchored by three enormous magnolias.

One of Emily Whaley's most distinctive and successful efforts in vernacular garden design is at the home of her daughter, Emily Wharton Whaley Whipple (Miss Em) at Yeamans Hall Club, which is about a thirty-minute drive into Berkeley County from downtown Charleston. Yeamans Hall Club was founded in 1925 by well-to-do northerners looking for a refuge from freezing cold, ice, and snow in the temperate climate of the South Carolina lowcountry. The property is largely undeveloped with a sprinkling of cottages well protected from each other. This rural estate descends from one of the very early Charleston area plantations with an original land grant from the English king. The property is bordered by Goose Creek and an immense marsh with one of nature's grandest "infinity views."

Yeamans Hall is one of the most remarkable garden spots in the United States with its unspoiled countryside, forests, dirt roads, marsh views, tidal creeks, heron, egret, migrating water fowl, and white-tailed deer. The historic clubhouse and dining facility are surrounded by a parklike English-style garden filled with azaleas, enormous camellias, and ancient live oaks. The locally acclaimed camellia breeder Sam Borom propagated and planted many of the camellias at Yeamans Hall and other lowcountry South Carolina gardens.

In September 1989 Hurricane Hugo snapped many old growth trees into pieces and played havoc with many lowcountry South Carolina gardens, including those at Yeamans Hall. Club member Roger Milliken (1915–2010) was there to spearhead the clean up and replanting of club property. The grounds committee of Yeamans Hall then directed that the undergrowth forests be cleared to enhance views from the miles of dirt roads that wind through the estate and further determined that additional water courses visible from the dirt roads needed to be created.

Emily Whaley looked at the devastation of Miss Em's fairly modest garden at Yeamans Hall after Hugo, and her face broke out into a smile, "Now, you can have a real garden—you have sunshine." Emily's plans for Miss Em's garden were always directed to accommodating Miss Em's wishes consistent with Emily's well-honed views about the appropriate ingredients of a great, small garden. Again and again Emily would say to Miss Em, "What do you want?" With the help of Junior (Cuffie Robinson), the beds were laid out, statues placed, and various shrubs, camellias, and azaleas planted. Then Miss Em's husband, Grant Dodge Whipple (1919–2006), designed and had laid out an irrigation system for the garden. But the most important thing Emily suggested to make Miss Em's garden a success was to "appropriate a borrowed view" of the immense Goose Creek marsh. Consequently the vista from Miss Em's Yeamans Hall home and garden, although quite different, is every bit as splendid as those at England's Stourhead and France's Vaux-le-Viscomte.

Emily Whaley believed that by gardening, the eye is trained to discover beauty. Her passion was to create a garden that was full of surprises and nuances. She wanted the viewer to be enveloped slowly and inescapably in a web of fragrance, sounds, color, and design. There were key elements that in her opinion were important in creating the perfect garden, a place for entertaining, pleasure, communing with the soul. She describes those elements in her opening essay.

Emily Whaley's rubrics for the creation of a great garden are by no way unique: the perfect design, screens for privacy, water as a mirror, focal points to draw the eye, borrowed vistas for drama, comfortable seating for relaxing, paths as routes for exploration, grass to contrast with flowers, and color and bloom at eye level. These provide a set of glasses for viewing the great gardens of the world.

Why do I love to visit gardens? Why do I love to garden? The parable of the men on safari provides one explanation. When I am in the midst of a sun-filled, fragrant garden, whether spring or fall, I forget time, forget the worries of the world, and become one with my surroundings. Recently I have been creating a new garden at our mountain house on Lake Summit, North Carolina. The challenge is finding the right design for an elliptical dell. And then there is the challenge of selecting and planting the perfect plants. The dell has lovely white crepe myrtles at one end, and thus white, with its magic lightness, prompted a selection of white hydrangeas for outlines. Yes, I love to garden. But, even more, I love to visit a well-maintained, unique garden here or in another culture. My hope is that you find in these essays and illustrations a starting point and a roadmap for some of your own garden adventures.

Fred and I recently saw a Green Planet television documentary on the construction of the Three Gorges Dam on the Yangtze River in China. The water level in the affected mountain valleys of the Yangtze has risen four hundred feet or more and has forced the abandonment of thousands of ancient villages, cities, farms, businesses, and homesteads and the relocation of inhabitants. The poignancy of the gut-wrenching losses of these structures, lands, and historical and religious sites tied so closely to the identities of the evacuees reminded me of the flooding of Belvidere in 1942, the year of my birth. The contrast is stark between the photographs in this epilogue of Belvidere Plantation House and of the author standing on the remains of the front steps to Belvidere during the drought of 2010. When the waters of Lake Marion receded and once again allowed visitation, the Sinkler and African American descendants went back to Belvidere to stand and picnic in what had once been the hallowed garden of their ancestors and to reaffirm their affection for a long-lost, beloved place and for each other.

Suggestions for Further Reading

Acton, Harold. *Memoirs of an Aesthete.* London: Hamish Hamilton Ltd., 1984.

Anderton, Stephen. *Discovering Welsh Gardens.* Cardiff, Wales: Graffeg, 2009.

Ball, Anne S. *Pinopolis: History of a Pineland Village.* Berkeley County, S.C.: privately printed, 1983.

Bennett, Paul. *The Garden Lover's Guide to the South.* New York: Princeton Architectural Press, 2000.

Berrall, Julia S. *The Garden: An Illustrated History.* New York: Viking Press, 1966.

Bertin, Philippe. *Normandy: Routes of Discovery.* Rennes, Fr.: Ouest-France, 2008.

Coats, Peter. *Great Gardens of the Western World.* New York: G. P. Putnam's Sons, 1963.

Coxe, Elizabeth Sinkler. *Tales from the Grand Tour, 1890–1910.* Ed. Anne Sinkler Whaley LeClercq. Columbia, S.C.: University of South Carolina Press, 2006.

Davis, Evangeline. *Charleston Houses and Gardens.* Charleston, S.C.: Preservation Society of Charleston, 1975.

Demoly, Jean-Pierre. *La Villa Ephrussi de Rothschild.* Paris: Les Éditions de l'Amateur, 2002.

Fishburne, Anne Sinkler. *Belvidere.* Columbia: University of South Carolina Press, 1950.

Greenoak, Francesca. *The Gardens of the National Trust for Scotland.* London: Aurum Press, 2005.

Haskell, Eric T. *The Gardens of Brécy: A Lasting Landscape.* Paris: Huitième Jour Éditions, 2007.

Hellyer, Arthur. *Gardens of Genius.* London: Hamlyn Publishing Group, 1980.

Hobhouse, Penelope. *Garden Style.* Boston: Little, Brown, 1988.

———. *Jardins d'Exception.* London: Frances Lincoln, 2006.

———. *The Garden Lover's Guide to Italy.* New York: Princeton Architectural Press, 1998.

Jekyll, Gertrude. *The Illustrated Gertrude Jekyll: Colour Schemes for the Flower Garden.* Boston: Little, Brown, 1988.

Keen, Mary. *Gardening with Color.* New York: Random House, 1991.

LeClercq, Anne Sinkler Whaley. *An Antebellum Plantation Household: Including the South Carolina Low Country Receipts and Remedies of Emily Wharton Sinkler.* Columbia: University of South Carolina Press, 1996.

———. *Between North and South.* Columbia: University of South Carolina Press, 2006.

Pozzana, Mariachiara. *Gardens of Florence and Tuscany: A Complete Guide.* Florence: Giunti Editore, 2001.

Plumptre, George. *Garden Ornament: Five Hundred Years of History and Practice.* New York: Thames and Hudson, 1998.

———. *Great Gardens, Great Designers.* London: Seven Dials, 1999.

Quest-Ritson, Charles. *The Garden Lover's Guide to Germany.* New York: Princeton Architectural Press, 1998.

Reeves-Smyth, Terrance. *The Garden Lover's Guide to Ireland.* New York: Princeton Architectural Press, 2001.

Rose, Graham. *The Romantic Garden.* New York: Penguin Books, 1988.

Segall, Barbara. *The Garden Lover's Guide to Spain and Portugal.* New York: Princeton Architectural Press, 1999.

Stevenson, Violet. *The Wild Garden.* New York: Penguin Books, 1985.

Tankard, Judith B., and Martin A. Wood. *Gertrude Jekyll at Munstead Wood.* Surrey, U.K.: Bramley Books, 1998.

Taylor, Patrick. *The Garden Lover's Guide to Britain.* New York: Princeton Architectural Press, 1998.

———. *The Garden Lover's Guide to France.* New York: Princeton Architectural Press, 1998.

Truscott, James. *Private Gardens of Scotland.* London: Weidenfeld and Nicolson, 1988.

Verey, Rosemary. *Classic Garden Design: How to Adapt and Recreate Garden Features of the Past.* New York: Congdon & Weed. 1984.

Walton, Susana. *La Mortella: An Italian Garden Paradise.* London: New Holland Publishers, 2002.

Whaley, Emily. *Mrs. Whaley and Her Charleston Garden.* Chapel Hill: Algonquin Books, 1997.

Index

Page numbers in italics refer to photographs.

About the Author

A native of Charleston, South Carolina, ANNE SINKLER WHALEY LECLERCQ has retired as the director of the Daniel Library at the Citadel. She holds a master's degree in librarianship from Emory University and a J.D. from the University of Tennessee. LeClercq is editor of *Between North and South: The Letters of Emily Wharton Sinkler, 1842–1865* and *Elizabeth Sinkler Coxe's Tales from the Grand Tour, 1890–1910,* and she is the author of *An Antebellum Plantation Household: Including the South Carolina Low Country Receipts and Remedies of Emily Wharton Sinkler.*